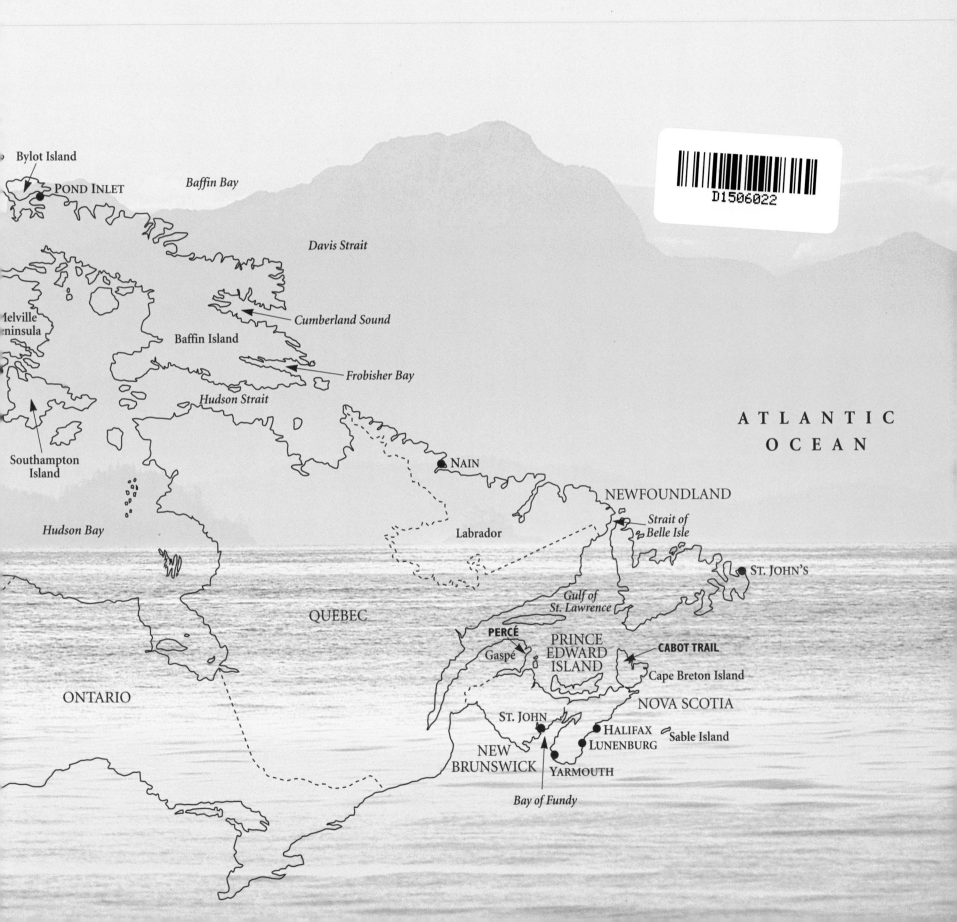

Bylot Island

Baffin Bay

POND INLET

Davis Strait

Melville Peninsula

Cumberland Sound

Baffin Island

Frobisher Bay

Hudson Strait

Southampton Island

Hudson Bay

NAIN

NEWFOUNDLAND

Strait of Belle Isle

Labrador

ATLANTIC OCEAN

ST. JOHN'S

Gulf of St. Lawrence

QUEBEC

PERCÉ

PRINCE EDWARD ISLAND

CABOT TRAIL

Gaspé

Cape Breton Island

NOVA SCOTIA

ONTARIO

ST. JOHN

HALIFAX

Sable Island

NEW BRUNSWICK

LUNENBURG

YARMOUTH

Bay of Fundy

SEACOASTS

SEACOASTS

PIERRE BERTON

PHOTOGRAPHS BY ANDRÉ GALLANT

Stoddart

Published in 1998 by
Stoddart Publishing Co. Limited
34 Lesmill Road, Toronto, Canada M3B 2T6
Tel. (416) 445-3333   Fax (416) 445-5967

Stoddart Books are available for bulk purchase for sales promotions,
premiums, fundraising, and seminars. For details,
contact the **Special Sales Department** at the above address.

Canadian Cataloguing in Publication Data
Berton, Pierre, 1920-
Seacoasts
ISBN 0-7737-3095-8

1. Coasts – Canada – History. 2. Coasts – Canada – Pictorial works.
3. Canada – History. 4. Canada – Pictorial works. 5. Canada – Social life and customs.
6. Canada – Social life and customs – Pictorial works. I. Gallant, André II. Title.

FC51.B47 1998   971'.00946   C98-930363-2   F1008.B47 1998

Film by Rainbow Digicolor Inc., Toronto

Printed in Singapore

CONTENTS

FROM SEA TO SHINING SEA

CANADA BOASTS THE LONGEST COASTLINE IN THE WORLD. IF IT WERE straightened out it could be wound around the equator three and a half times and there would still be a bit left over. It is a paradox that although we are surrounded on three sides by salt water, we do not think of ourselves as a maritime people. Nor are we judged as such by the rest of the world. It's what lies between the coasts that matters more. The provender of the sea—from the Pacific's tinned salmon to the Atlantic's salt cod—has long been a factor in our export trade, but our biggest staple products, wheat, lumber, pulpwood, and minerals, come from the hinterland.

We are not fish eaters—unlike the Portuguese who plundered so much of our cod before the two-hundred-mile limit was invoked. I can remember when Toronto had only one seafood restaurant. Today there are more: chefs throw a few shrimps on top of a piece of Alberta beef and call it Surf and Turf. But this remains a meat-and-potatoes country.

We do not have a merchant marine worthy of the name, though we once did during the great age of sail and again during the Second World War. Although one of the world's great shipping lines had its birth on our Atlantic shores, it is the railway linking the two coasts that has given us our defining moment.

The beauty and the majesty of the sea surrounds us on three sides, offering a rich and varied landscape of fiords and inlets, salt marshes and tidal mudflats, sandbars and tombolos, pebbled beaches, spits, berms, and marine cliffs—washed, scoured, and half drowned by the tides and the vagrant winds. Occasionally grotesque, often terrifying, always enchanting, the sea has been a paradise for photographers and a mecca for sightseers.

That is how the first arrivals saw the new land—a mysterious seagirt realm stretching back from the coastal mists into the unknown. What a mixed bag of seafarers they were—stocky Siberians and haughty Spaniards; dour

Scottish traders and polished British naval officers; Portuguese fishermen, Viking wanderers, French merchants, and, for all we know, Irish monks in skin boats and Chinese merchants blown off course far from familiar shores. They were searching for refuge, for safe harbours protected by rockbound cliffs and islands, often near the mouths of great rivers. How could they divine that in the distant future these would be the sites of populous cities?

Thus, our earliest history is tied to our coastlines. But it is not the balmy Pacific that gives us an international image, nor the rugged Atlantic shore. We are seen—properly, I think—as a northern nation, and it is the Arctic coastline and the vision of the remarkable aboriginals who exist along its shores that intrigue the armchair traveller.

Since Elizabethan times we have mined the coastal shallows of a treasure we believed to be limitless. The early explorers gave no thought to the future. Why should they? There was a time when the coastal waters teemed with so many fish that, it is said, they were compelled to slow their ships in order to force their way through.

This book is being published at a time when the East Coast cod and the West Coast salmon are each facing the possibility of something close to extinction. The only reason why we did not lose them decades ago is that we had not yet devised the technical ability to destroy them in quantity. Now, at last, our ingenuity has caught up with our greed.

Have we learned nothing from the past? Not a great deal, when one recalls the near extinction of the sea otter in the Pacific and the bowhead whale in the Arctic. It has become increasingly difficult in the modern world to ignore the demands of commerce in the interests of conservation. The history of these crenellated coasts tells us that we must begin to resist those demands, painful though the prospect may be.

Fishing house, Sointula, Malcolm Island, Queen Charlotte Strait, B.C.

Inside Passage near Port Hardy, B.C.

Freighter off Stanley Park, Vancouver, B.C.

Shoreline, Pond Inlet, Baffin Island.

Nain, Labrador coast.

Potato field, Stanley Bridge, P.E.I.

The rocks at Hopewell Cape, Bay of Fundy, N.B.

The Battery, St. John's, Newfoundland

Imperial Eagle Channel, Vancouver Island.

THE PACIFIC COAST

IF THE PEOPLE OF THE PACIFIC COAST THINK OF THEMSELVES AS "DIFFER-ent"—and they do—it's partly because the Pacific littoral is a separate world. My friend the novelist and naturalist Fred Bodsworth has called it an "invisible cage," its apartness illustrated as much by what it keeps out as by what it keeps in. White spruce and trembling aspen have rarely invaded this closed world; poison ivy, red raspberry, and sumach are unknown, and so are the common crow and the meadow mouse. Inside the cage flourish the broad-leafed arbutus and Victoria's singular Garry oak. British Columbia's emblem, the flowering dogwood, is unique to the Pacific.

The cage stretches north from Vancouver Island to beyond the lonely Queen Charlottes. To the west, a frieze of offshore islands—6,500 of them—protects the Inside Passage. To the east, separated by the long underwater trench known as the Coastal Trough, the mountains, riven by glacial fjords, drop perpendicularly to the water. The Pacific shelf is only one-sixth as wide as its Atlantic counterpart, but the coastline is the longest in Canada: 550 miles from Washington State to the Alaskan Panhandle, but 15,500 if you unravel it.

This is a domain of superlatives. The mountains are the highest, the trees among the oldest and tallest, the rainfall the greatest on the continent. (When you open your front door there's one chance in three you'll need an umbrella.) The glaciers that once covered the mainland were so huge they compressed the land 820 feet or more. When they melted, all but the highest points of the Gulf Islands were drowned by the sea.

When the land sprang back, tons of sediment were released into the valleys so that even today the Fraser River annually carries twenty million tons of mud, sand, and silt into the delta, a boon to Vancouver's market gardeners.

With mingled scorn and envy we Easterners look on the Pacific coast as a kind of lotus land, a laid-back region where the beaches are always crowded and everybody seems to own a boat. It was ever thus. Long before the European invasion, the aboriginals enjoyed the bounty of the sea and forest. The white men thought them lazy, but this favoured people had no need of Calvinist toil. That helps explain why the modern lotus-eaters reject, also with both scorn and envy, the Eastern "rat race."

CHAPTER ONE

THE POTLATCH PEOPLE

OME THIRTEEN THOUSAND YEARS AGO, WHEN THE FIRST HUMANS REACHED the New World, most of the land was entombed in a glacier so monstrous that it had sucked the shallower seas dry. Thus was created the land bridge that turned North America and Asia into geographic Siamese twins, joined at the head by the emerging land mass we call Beringia.

The newcomers were Siberians. We know this because the shamanistic rituals practised by the Pacific coast tribes at the time of the first European contact were almost identical to those practised in Siberia today. New research into the dental characteristics of the two peoples has further confirmed the connection.

The Siberians came in waves, moving up the unglaciated valley of the lower Yukon. Modern research rejects the concept of an ice-free corridor through the heart of the interior and suggests that they explored the Pacific coast in skin boats. With the glaciers receding, these were unstable times. The climate was warmer and drier than it is today. The salinity of the ocean was such that shellfish could not flourish in the bays and inlets, while the land, rebounding from the pressure of the ice, inhibited the spawning cycle of the salmon.

The descendants of the Siberian immigrants were a nomadic people—hunters of game and gatherers of wild berries. They became fishers and settled in villages only when the environment stabilized around 3500 B.C.

OPPOSITE: A cluster of Haida mortuary poles at Ninstints, now a World Heritage Site in the Queen Charlottes. Hollowed out at the top and ravaged by the elements, they hold the grave boxes of ancestral chiefs.

RIGHT: Edward Curtis, a pioneer photographer of the West Coast natives, made this study of a Kwakiutl chief and his party in a canoe carved from a cedar trunk.

Now the bounty of the ocean provided them with a leisure society unlike any other in the Americas. The peoples of the Pacific coast, like those in leisure societies elsewhere (the Athenian, for example), developed a high culture over several millennia because they had plenty of time on their hands. During the summer months they exploited the immensely rich provender of the sea, devising a technology of nets and fish hooks, floats, traps, spears, lines, lures, and harpoons. The ocean was so richly endowed, the salmon runs so predictable, the means of fishing so efficient that the coastal natives could count on five work-free winter months in which to indulge in a burst of creative activity.

Thus winter became a ceremonial season—a time when the spiritual world melded with the natural world, when mythical beings lurked invisibly in the ever-green jungle, when the relatives of the dead donned special mourning masks in their memory, when spirit whistles and strange rattles could be heard in the forest,

A traditional Haida village, Masset, at the top of the Queen Charlotte archipelago, as it looked in the nineteenth century.

when dancing societies took over from the kinship societies of summertime. So great was this seasonal change that people abandoned their secular summer names and adopted new ones, tied to the winter ceremonials.

They lived on the margins of the rain forest, that gloomy and mysterious realm carpeted with creeping mosses and the cadavers of fallen trees from whose rotting bark new saplings grew and flourished. Under the canopy of the old-growth forest there existed, and still exists, a unique insect world—an isolated biological preserve that one writer has called "a sort of treetop Galapagos." The canopy itself harbours at least five hundred different insects, half of them species never before described. On the ground below another two thousand species live and thrive. From the forest floor rise the great evergreen giants—Douglas fir, Sitka spruce, western hemlock, red cedar—some soaring above the forest canopy as high as a modern fifty-storey skyscraper. These trees are the Methuselahs of the arboreal world. When Columbus reached America, there were trees on the Pacific coast that had been seedlings when Christ was born.

Let us try to imagine how the early aboriginals viewed these forest giants. A young man, say, leaves his coastal village and ventures into the mystic embrace of the evergreen world. What does he see? Just as Michelangelo saw the body of his David encased in a misshapen block of Carrara marble, so does this young man discern the shape of a gigantic canoe imprisoned within the trunk of a red cedar. Thus, the brooding presence of the rain forest is at the heart of the Pacific coast culture.

Bill Helen, a Tsimshian who at age thirty-five built his own forty-two-foot canoe from a nine-hundred-year-old red cedar, has put it eloquently:

"In building a canoe, we're passing on a life form from the forest and re-shaping it so that we can transport ourselves in it. It will be a vessel of aesthetics as well as functional. It has so much more use than any other piece of artwork. . . Once you get the log in the ocean, what's it going to do? We're taking this tree that was close to the end of its life and carrying this life along. I'll always envision this beautiful cedar tree out in the forest and it had its destiny, and its destiny was to be a part of history. It's got a life, it's got a character all its own. . ."

To the men who carve it and those who travel in it, everything in the canoe has a spiritual connection. That is why the carver puts a "heart" in his canoe—usually a protrusion carved out of the bow, with an eye painted on each side so the canoe always knows where it's going. Only in the spectral environment of the rain forest can a canoe have a spirit.

Like the salmon, the cedar tree sustained the early coastal tribes. The soft wood split easily into planks for the tribes' great low-pitched houses, some of them a

When Columbus reached America, there were trees on the Pacific coast that had been seedlings when Christ was born.

hundred feet long and big enough to shelter an extended family of more than twenty people. The aboriginals used every scrap of the tree: the bark and the roots were woven or plaited into clothing, blankets, and even waterproof containers.

The same techniques used to carve the early canoes and later animalistic figures were also used to carve and paint the vast cedar houses, that so astonished the early explorers. Simon Fraser paced off the size of a Salish house near the present site of Vancouver and reckoned it to be 150 feet long and ninety feet wide. Alexander Mackenzie, coming down the Bella Coola River in 1793, found houses with cedar boards so neatly joined they seemed to be all of one piece. As Robert McGhee, a Canadian archaeologist, has written, the coastal peoples must be placed among the greatest woodworkers in history. Their culture reached its zenith with the development of brightly painted heraldic poles—the "totem poles" that have become a kind of West Coast trademark.

ABOVE: Mountains of Hudson's Bay blankets—virtually legal tender among the nineteenth-century coast tribes—are piled up in a native house waiting for the coming potlatch.

RIGHT: Thick mosses shroud the rain forest on Kunghit Island off Queen Charlotte Sound.

By the time the first Europeans reached the coast by sea, these master woodworkers had developed a complex technology. Their tools included knives, adzes, and chisels of polished jade, wedges of wood or antler, drills with bone or stone points, and smaller implements made from the sharp teeth of the larger rodents.

Everything bore the imprint of the carver's knife—a canoe, a house, a post, a totem pole, a mask. James Cook, the first European to walk through a coastal village, was impressed by the ceremonial masks worn by the Nootka chiefs who greeted him in 1778. "If travelers . . . or voyageurs in an ignorant or credulous age had seen a number of people decorated in this manner, they would readily have believed . . . that there existed a race of beings partaking of the nature of man and beast," he wrote.

That visit was the start of what another writer has called, in a different context, "the fatal impact." George Vancouver, who had sailed as a midshipman under Cook, reached the Pacific coast in 1792 under orders to survey every foot of the wrinkled shoreline in an attempt to find an entrance to the fabled Northwest Passage. The meticulous seaman carried out his orders to the last inch, and although no passage was found, his accomplishments were remarkable. A more volatile man than Cook, he was not loved but certainly admired for that four-and-a-half-year surveying expedition—the longest in history.

The arrival of the Europeans touched off the explosive but short-lived sea-otter trade—a trade controlled not by avaricious whites but by equally avaricious Indians. It stands as a horrible example of how a great natural resource can, in a little more than half a century, be virtually wiped out by a surfeit of greed.

In 1778 after Cook anchored in Nootka Sound for a month of refitting, his crews obtained a number of sea-otter skins from the Indians. To their subsequent delight, they discovered that the pelts were highly prized in China, where they could be sold for as much as a hundred dollars apiece. In 1785 the first trading vessels reached Nootka and the rush was on for "soft gold." That same year an English trader, Alexander Walker, commented in his journal that the traders were so "craving and repacious" [*sic*] that "numbers of the Animal will be reduced and less valuable Skins brought to the market." No one heeded Walker; indeed, some traders attempted to make the skins more valuable by reducing the sea otter population. Between 1785 and 1825 no fewer than 330 ships were involved. Five years later the sea otter was virtually extinct along the Pacific coast.

Throughout that forty-year period the sea-otter trade brought new prosperity to the coastal tribes who had already been blessed by the largesse of forest and sea. Early on, the natives turned out to be experienced and skilful traders. Not for them the usual handfuls of baubles and beads. What they wanted were sophisticated iron implements, found to be so important for a woodworking culture. In some instances iron chisels became the standard medium of exchange.

Their hard bargaining caused prices to skyrocket. In 1788, members of Captain John Meares's crew had been able to buy ten skins for a single piece of copper. By 1792 the price had increased tenfold. In short, the stereotype of the greedy white traders cheating the aboriginals with trinkets and a few yards of cloth was turned upside down by the shrewd coastal tribesmen.

There was also a darker, more deadly side to the European invasion. The white seamen brought smallpox and venereal disease with them. By the mid-1860s, one-third of the native population of the Pacific coast had succumbed. By the early

An enormous hoard of flour in sacks is piled up at Alert Bay, off the Vancouver Island coast, waiting to be dispensed or destroyed in a potlatch.

1920s, after the impact of the Spanish influenza, epidemic there were only a quarter as many natives on the coast as there had been at the time of the first white contact. The Haida of the Queen Charlotte Islands were especially vulnerable; their number dropped from more than seven thousand to fewer than six hundred.

Equally devastating were the activities of the Christian missionaries who, supported by Indian agents in British Columbia, managed to persuade the government of John A. Macdonald in 1885 to ban the potlatch ceremony, the core of the culture of all tribes. It was a brutal, insensitive act—as devastating as if an alien invader had ordered the Roman Catholic clergy to cease holding high mass under pain of imprisonment.

A potlatch could last for several days and was sometimes years in the making. The ceremony validated status and rank and established claims to power and privilege. Only in a society as wealthy as that of the Pacific coast could such an affair have been possible, for it involved the giving away and even the destruction of personal property—for instance, thousands of sacks of flour would be chopped open and thrown into the ocean. With the coming of the white man, the Hudson's Bay blanket became the standard by which personal wealth was measured—the Indian equivalent of folding money—and was used as an economic yardstick in determining the comparative grandeur of a potlatch.

The brilliance of the Kwakiutl carvers can be seen on the painted cedar slab dwellings of this nineteenth-century village.

With increasing profits from the sea-otter trade bolstering an already affluent society, the potlatches of the early 1800s grew more and more sumptuous. The purpose was to demonstrate the host's superiority and to raise his social status. In 1803, Maquinna, the hereditary chief of the Nootka, held a potlatch in which he gave away two hundred muskets, two hundred yards of cloth, one hundred chemises, looking-glasses, and seven barrels of gun powder. These figures seem modest when set against the statistics of later years.

The parallels with the excesses of the European nobility are obvious. In the same century, the Duke of Sutherland gave a party on the Nile in honour of Albert, Prince of Wales. The liquid provisions placed aboard the steamer included three thousand bottles of champagne, four thousand bottles of wines and liquors, and twenty thousand bottles of soda water. But the duke's extravagance pales when compared with that of the later Pacific coast potlatches. There the nobility was recklessly profligate. As the potlatches became more and more extravagant, some chiefs were bankrupted and even driven to suicide by their attempts to keep up with the neighbours. In the first half of the nineteenth century the largest of the potlatches saw the equivalent of 320 blankets given away. In twenty years' time the equivalent of nine thousand blankets was dispensed at a single potlatch. By 1895 the number had risen to thirteen thousand.

Even this seems minor when compared to the last great potlatch given in 1921 by Chief Daniel Cranmer of the Nimkish. The chief had devoted eight years of hard work and trading to achieve this memorable ceremony at which the equivalent of thirty thousand blankets was distributed. Besides the actual blankets given away at this six-day feast, the presents included canoes, motorboats, pool tables, oak trunks, violins, guitars, sewing machines, gramophones, bedsteads, bureaus, washtubs, crockery, and a thousand sacks of flour as well as coins flung about for the delight of the children.

By this time, of course, the potlatch had been declared illegal. The RCMP arrived, spirited the chief off to jail, and seized whatever presents they could, including twenty-three "coppers"—the highly prized and expensive shields of beaten metal displayed at potlatches to emphasize their owner's wealth. These were never returned but can be seen today at the Museum of Civilization in Hull.

Cranmer emerged from jail broke but unrepentant. "Everybody admits it was the biggest yet," he said triumphantly. "In the old days this was my weapon. I could call down anyone." "Calling down"—the phrase is reminiscent of a Hollywood western—became the ultimate aim. To offer a guest a shield of beaten copper was a challenge that could not be refused. He must return an equally valuable copper to retain his status in the community; if he couldn't afford it, he was a figure of shame.

Some of the reasons advanced for outlawing the potlatch were spurious. (The ceremony disrupted the school year, it was argued. And it wasn't healthful because the celebrants consumed far too much rich food.) The truth was that the white Europeans could not abide a culture that seemed to them to be not only a waste of time but also a waste of resources. The system was based on the hoarding of goods, not for savings and investment, but for seemingly senseless waste.

In short, the coastal tribes, in refusing to act like white men, had rejected the Protestant work ethic. As an Indian commissioner wrote, "it is not possible that Indians can acquire property or become industrious with any good result while under the influence of this mania."

Government policy had been to "improve" the Indians by assimilation. The Indians—especially the Kwakiutl—resisted. For this they were damned by government agents and missionaries as "incorrigible," "intractable," "a bad set," and "a most difficult lot to civilize."

"They appear to desire to resist, so to speak, the inroads of civilization on old savage customs," British Columbia's superintendent of Indian affairs declared in 1883. As far as the federal department was concerned, the Kwakiutl remained "antagonistic toward the white race" and "opposed to anything and everything advanced by the white man." One group of elders told an Indian agent that they might as well die as give up the potlatch. When the Kwakiutl found they could not persuade the authorities to rescind the law, they continued to hold potlatches in secret.

Some of these clandestine potlatches were disguised as Christmas feasts or Yuletide holiday giving. Others were held in places so inaccessible that no one could approach the site without being seen. In 1931, the "disjointed potlatch" was devised. By splitting the ancient rite into two parts—one a ceremony for gift-giving, the other for dancing—the Indians made it hard for the authorities to connect the two.

The Kwakiutl closed ranks, remaining as tight-lipped as any Mafioso invoking the law of *omertà*. The police found themselves up against a stone wall, as one constable admitted. The Indians themselves made it clear that anyone who informed would become an outcast.

By 1933, as one agent reported to Victoria, his position had become intolerable; at this point the potlatch had reached a zenith not approached in years and the Indians had become "bolder and quite open in carrying it out." After that the authorities left them alone. In 1951 the law was revised and the potlatch again went public. It became a shorter and more informal festival but one still replete with the masks and dances that were an essential part of the artistic renaissance that marked the mid-twentieth century. In the long struggle to save their culture from being smothered by that of an alien invader, the Indians had clearly won.

A veritable fortune in Hudson's Bay blankets attested to the wealth of the chief who gave them away. This photograph was taken in Fort Rupert in 1894.

THE QUEEN CHARLOTTES

Called Gwaii Haanas by the Haida, they are among the most isolated islands in Canada. They number more than 150 and are biologically unique, a Canadian version of Darwin's famous Galapagos, with rare plants and even some animal subspecies not found anywhere else on the continent.

Moresby Island, home of the Haida and scene of a long struggle with logging interests, is now the site of Canada's 33rd national park.

The narrow Skidegate channel cuts through the island complex between Graham Island and Moresby.

Gwaii Haanas, a national park reserve, has become a mecca for biologists and conservationists concerned to protect the last of the decaying totem poles and the vanishing rain forest.

Here, in the land of the bald eagles, is the second largest archipelago in Canada. Protected by the sea when the ice swept down to cover most of the country, the islands were linked to the mainland as the water was drained from Hecate Strait. To this sheltered paradise, some eight thousand years ago, came the ancestors of the gifted artists and carvers who still call it home. It is geologically unstable with more earthquakes than any other part of Canada, caused by the movement of tectonic plates.

South Moresby National Park encompasses 138 islands and 42 freshwater lakes. These are the Gordon Islands near the southern tip, not far from Ninstints.

LEFT: *Sunset at Masset, the ancient Haida community at the northern tip of the Gwaii Haanas archipelago.*

TOP: *Yellow potentilla, also known as cinquefoil, a member of the rose family, brightens Reef Island's rocks.*

RIGHT: *Low tide on one of Graham Island's rock-strewn beaches.*

CHAPTER TWO

WHAT HAPPENED TO THE SALMON?

I T IS AUGUST 18, 1978, AND I AM LOLLING ON A DECK CHAIR AT THE STERN OF HAL Straight's big boat, mooching for coho. We are anchored off the Sunshine Coast, not far from the resort town of Sechelt, and the waters seem to be alive with salmon. We can see them on the radar screen and judge their depth with the sonar—modern devices that have made salmon fishing perhaps a little too easy for the fisherman.

Mooching is a lazy man's sport, perfectly adapted to the laid-back lifestyle of the Pacific coast. My rod sits in its holder, the leaded line baited with wriggling herring and dropped to the requisite depth, waiting for a fish.

Suddenly, the shrill whine of the reel—*zinggg!*—rouses me from my torpor. A fish has struck. I seize the rod and struggle to keep the line taut as the coho—a flash of silver—leaps from the water a hundred yards distant.

He's trying to snap the line, and I won't let him. I reel in fast, then let the line slacken for a moment as he turns and bolts. The tussle continues, back and forth. He tries to get under the boat. I forestall him. He circles it warily, but I keep up with him. In the end he tangles the line round the outboard, snaps it, and vanishes.

I've lost him, but it doesn't matter. There are plenty more fish in the sea: always have been, always will be—or so we believe. Not just coho but its commercial cousins, chum, pink, and sockeye, which together form the backbone of the flourishing B.C. canning industry, and, of course, that other great sport fish the spring salmon, variously known as the king, the tyee, and the chinook. The spring doesn't fight the way the smaller coho does. Instead, it runs, forcing the fisher to pay out miles of line as it tries to break free. Once when we anchored in a sheltering bay, we left one baited hook in the water while we went ashore for a snack. When we returned we discovered that a big spring had taken the bait and then circled the harbour three or four times, tying it up like a Christmas parcel.

We hauled in that exhausted fish. We lost several others, but losing a fish in those days was not a tragedy. Once, I remember, three of my kids and I put out from Galiano Island in a borrowed boat and in just forty-five minutes pulled a twenty-five-pound spring from the roiling waters of Active Pass.

Back in 1905, when the photograph opposite was taken, it was no problem to trap these huge chinooks.

In those heady days there seemed no end to this great natural resource. Scores of canneries were shipping B.C. salmon, especially sockeye, around the world. Canned salmon became an international favourite, from lunch pail to canapé tray. Greater and greater quantities of salmon were being hauled out of the ocean by a

growing fleet of commercial fishing boats. In a single decade—1975–85—the annual catch tripled. Then, with a suddenness that seems cataclysmic, the bubble burst. The glory days were gone.

In the early 1990s sports and commercial fishermen awoke to the startling news that some varieties of Pacific salmon might be facing extinction. By the autumn of 1994 it was clear that something was terribly wrong. Millions of salmon—perhaps as many as 3.2 million—were missing from two major runs on the Fraser River. The blame rested squarely on the shoulders of the federal department of fisheries and oceans, which, in 1992, had suffered budget cuts and a reorganization that demoralized staff. Two problems were evident. The department not only was lax in its supervision but also didn't have an accurate method of counting fish. Its earlier optimistic estimates of the numbers of salmon available encouraged overfishing. Because of the apparent glut of salmon the season wasn't closed until the last minute—to the point where one migration came within twelve hours of being wiped out. Nor had the department been able to control extensive poaching on the river.

That there were fewer salmon available was undeniable. For years the annual catch had averaged twenty-seven million. By 1996 it had shrunk to little more than seven million. In the Strait of Georgia, the coho, too, seemed to have vanished. Every April the fisheries department has made a preliminary survey of coho catches. Normally, in this early month, the number had averaged about thirteen thousand, a clear sign that millions more would follow as the season reached its peak. But in 1997 the coho just weren't there. The statistics were devastating. In the month of April only *thirteen* coho—not thirteen thousand—were caught in those same shimmering waters where I had once lolled at my ease, secure in the knowledge that a fish would strike.

To comprehend what was happening it is necessary to understand something about the mysterious, romantic, and ultimately tragic life span of these noble fish. For them the colour of death is not black but crimson. At spawning time, when their silver scales lose their lustre and their flesh changes to a different hue, the rivers that empty into the sea are the colour of blood. I remember hiking along one of these blood-red rivers—the Goldstream on Vancouver Island—in the Depression days (when salmon were so plentiful and cheap they sold for twenty-five cents a pound); the fish were packed so tightly in their struggle it seemed one could cross from shore to shore on their backs.

It is this frantic obsession to force their way upstream to the gravels of their birthplace that distinguishes the Pacific salmon. On their long odyssey the fish change shape as well as colour, their snouts erupting and humps appearing on the backs of the males. Are these changes designed to increase their sexual attractiveness? We cannot be certain, but we do know that on this perilous migration, where they leap waterfalls and batter themselves in the rapids and among the rocks, they take no food, relying on their reserves of fat for energy.

Life for these salmon is an especial tragedy, for the mating call that drives them on is also a funeral dirge. It ends after a few hours of sexual frenzy as male and female, quivering side by side in a nest gouged from the streambed, simultaneously release hundreds of eggs and clouds of sperm. Within a week, exhausted, bruised, and listless, they drift downstream to die.

I have gazed on one of these spent salmon, purchased from a group of Han Indians on the upper Yukon, and have marvelled at its long journey of more than six hundred miles from tidewater. What mysterious force had reached out to it and to thousands of its fellows somewhere in the depths of the Pacific? What had turned their faces simultaneously to our coasts? Was it, as some suggest, electro-magnetic fields generated by currents and tides? Was it traces of fresh water encountered far out in the ocean? Had the salmon somehow managed to smell out the mouths of the rivers and follow that scent to within a few feet of their hatching places? These explanations sound nonsensical, but no more unreasonable than the seven-mile current of the great river they encountered from Norton Sound to Carmacks. Somehow this magnificent fish, now sizzling over a wood fire, had managed to cover as much as eighty-seven miles a day in its search for the spawning grounds that it had left four or five years before.

Today its kind is threatened with extinction. What went wrong?

A variety of reasons has been advanced—everything from climatic changes to logging practices. But the chief reason can be boiled down to a single word: greed. Too many people took too great an unthinking advantage of the sea's bounty and all but destroyed it. Conservation measures were rarely discussed in the glory days, and those that were adopted were scarcely onerous. Off the Sunshine Coast in the seventies and eighties, four of us could easily catch our limit in a few hours—sixteen fish a day, from one boat. The number of fish caught was actually increasing in those days; nobody seemed alarmed that the *weight* of the annual harvest had declined. The average sizes of all five species dropped as fishing pressure increased.

In the days before the Europeans arrived, the various aboriginal tribes along the coast maintained strict rules to protect the fish stocks. When commercial fishing

Life for these salmon is an especial tragedy, for the mating call that drives them on is also a funeral dirge.

began in British Columbia in the last century it did so in an atmosphere that encouraged waste. A century and a half ago the great spring salmon (or chinook) was the basis of the canning industry. But to net a chinook the fishers were forced to net other species of salmon, all of which were clubbed to death and flung back into the water. In one single month—May 1877—ten thousand Fraser River sockeye were destroyed as unmarketable in the nets of the pioneer canner Alexander Ewen. In a letter (signed "Sockeye") to the press of the day, one writer referred to "the presence of floating masses of putrid carcasses which have been polluting every arm of the river from the city to the Gulf."

The sockeye came into its own about that time, when the canners realized that they could sell it overseas as easily as the chinook (the pink and the chum continued to be wasted for the next twenty years). At the peak of the run there was such a glut of salmon that the canneries could not handle them all; the New Westminster *Columbian* reported that as many as five thousand dead fish were dumped in a single day. Only the choice bits of the sockeye were canned; at least a third and, during the peak of the run, as much as a half of the fish was thrown away to pollute the river.

The profligate attitude to a major natural resource continued for most of the next century. Profit, not conservation, has always been at the root of government and industry policy on the West Coast. For years the fishermen's union (UFAWU) had urged a limit on the number of licences issued, not so much to protect the fish as to protect the incomes of the fishers. Similarly, the canners' chief concerns had nothing to do with protecting the stock; it was the price of the fish they wanted to protect.

When in 1968 the federal fisheries minister, Jack Davis, unveiled his plan for limiting licences, he made little pretence that conservation was the issue. Instead, he talked of "measures to increase the earning power of B.C. salmon fishermen." Nor was there much suggestion that the total catch be reduced. As Geoff Meggs, the leading historian of the salmon's decline, has pointed out, the Davis plan represented "the triumph of those who believed the salmon fishery was simply a question of producing money from fish."

The large rivers have long been the subject of public attention. On the Fraser, for example, fish ladders installed at Hell's Gate aided the salmon in their long homeward quest. But British Columbia's vaunted industrial progress is such that only a few conservationists have cared about the innumerable small streams heedlessly destroyed by mining and logging interests. As one writer for *Nature Canada* has pointed out, even if fishing magically ended tomorrow, the salmon would still be in trouble.

In pre-war days Japanese women worked in the B.C. canneries, filling tins with sockeye while carrying their babies on their backs.

Urbanization is one culprit for which there is no cure. The Gulf of Georgia harbours the spawning grounds for half the salmon entering the strait. Unfortunately, this is also the fastest-growing section of the province. Its human population of five million is expected to double by 2018. The spawning grounds are becoming victims of the bulldozer because, as Dan Edwards, a third-generation commercial fisherman, has said, "subdivisions are generally more profitable than salmon streams."

To save the Pacific salmon drastic measures have been proposed and, in some cases, implemented; they include cutting the fishing fleet in half, reducing the number of licences, and even putting a moratorium on catching certain species, such as the chinook. But with thousands of jobs at stake, is salvation politically possible? Would the government be prepared to pay compensation? Biologists have criticized government policies as half measures, but even tepid conservation methods can be costly. Since 1992 they have cost the troll fleet an additional fifty million dollars.

A real concern is that a good many members of the industry have given up on the Pacific salmon. Fish farming in British Columbia was launched in 1984. Within a decade 75 percent of the salmon raised on farms were an imported species—the Atlantic salmon, which gains weight faster than its Pacific cousin and is easier to control. The salmon farms have become the largest agricultural exporters in the province, employing 2,400 people at some ninety sites.

This unregulated explosion of fish farms has a down side. As anybody knows, the introduction of an exotic species almost always plays hob with the native. The introduction of rabbits into Australia, of goats to the Galapagos Islands, and of Canadian beaver into Patagonia was disastrous to local species. It is virtually impossible to confine the new salmon to the pens. And Atlantic salmon have already been found in twenty-one river systems in British Columbia. A freak storm in July 1996 caused one hundred thousand of these rogue salmon to escape. Almost certainly this new species will introduce new diseases and weaken the genetic integrity of the native fish. The problem is ballooning. Already the total population of farmed fish surpasses that of their wild cousins.

Does it matter? Of course it does. It matters to those of us who have dipped our lines in the cold Pacific waters; who have heard the familiar *zing!* as the reel comes alive; whose hearts have leaped with the silver flash of the coho; who have seen the rivers crimson with gasping sockeye or chinook; who have gazed on the forest of the salmon fleet's masts at Steveston, or watched the great fish drying on the natives' racks on the high banks of the Yukon.

But it actually matters to us all, for this is the bounty we inherited—sportsmen, trollers, packers alike. *Tame* salmon? On the Pacific coast that is an oxymoron. Let us leave the final word to Eric Bonham of the Urban Stream Stewardship Program, who understands the mystic link between fish and fisher and who is trying to protect the vanishing habitats by forging a partnership between government and concerned citizens. "What we are trying to do," he has said, "is to build and re-establish a lasting relationship between people and the salmon. We do not seem to realize that if we destroy the salmon we are also destroying ourselves."

Soldering vent holes in salmon tins after the air has been removed (c.1913).

THE DAYS WHEN SALMON WAS KING

These incredible photographs from a bygone era only hint at the vast quantities of salmon available in a single day to one cannery on the Fraser. With catches like these, the supply seemed inexhaustible.

ABOVE: Trapped alive, these salmon were brailed (hauled in) from the traps to be deposited, wriggling, into the hold.

RIGHT: This was only part of an evening's catch on the Fraser — destined for the Anglo-B.C. Packing Company's Phoenix cannery.

ABOVE: *Fishing boats queue up at B.C. Canneries, waiting to unload their salmon.*

LEFT: *The painstaking chore of mending nets.*

RIGHT: *With their boat loaded with the day's catch, fishermen haul up a salmon trap.*

ABOVE: Chinese workers cleaning salmon at a New Westminster cannery in 1887.

RIGHT: In a Fraser delta cannery, two Chinese workers take a brief break.

OPPOSITE: This was the scene in 1898 at Steveston in the delta when the big square-riggers loaded up with cases of tinned salmon for delivery around Cape Horn to Great Britain and Europe.

These photographs give a good idea of the great salmon glut that provided thousands of jobs for British Columbians before overfishing reduced the catch. This is the front dock of the Imperial Cannery at Richmond in the 1940s when the harbours were jammed with boats and the boats crammed with fish.

CHAPTER THREE

KEEPERS OF THE LIGHT

*Built in 1860, the Fisgard Lighthouse at the entrance to
Victoria's Esquimalt Harbour was the first on the B.C. coast.*

OH, FOR THE LIFE OF A LIGHTHOUSE KEEPER! FREED FROM THE HUMDRUM existence of the urban toiler, he enjoys a life of romance and adventure. He is his own boss; he sets his hours of work without interference; no superior creatures lurk in the next office. He is lord of all he surveys, alone, with the salt spray of the sea in his nostrils, protected from the cacophony of modern living, supreme in his isolation from the cares of the contemporary world. And how comforting it is to know that the lives of shipwrecked people are in his hands! To them he can be a saviour.

Some prospective custodians have believed this myth. Others, after a lifetime spent on a rocky shoreline, have felt a real sense of accomplishment. There are still one or two who, having longed for a hermit-like existence, have achieved it and revelled in it.

But these belonged to a minority of romantics and loners. In the mid-1980s Donald Graham, a B.C. writer, himself a former lightkeeper, shattered the myth in two volumes dealing with the lighthouses of the Pacific coast. Based on official correspondence and on personal interviews, the two books present a litany of misery. Graham's meticulous research tells a different tale: of penny-pinching governments that kept the lightkeepers in a state of penury and debt; of men and women driven to insanity by the isolation; of injury and even suicide brought about by the appalling conditions they endured.

Consider the case of James Henry Sadler, one of the horrible examples unearthed by Graham. Sadler took over the Kains Island light on Quatsino Sound in November 1915, only to learn that his total pay would be a mere forty dollars a month. He hadn't had enough funds to buy a three-month supply of food and was forced to persuade a Victoria wholesaler to cash his quarterly paycheque. On Kains, Salder, his wife, and his three small children were almost entirely cut off from the world. Just to get his mail he was forced to row seventeen miles to Winter Harbour and then row another seventeen miles back. The federal marine department refused to pay the five dollars it would have cost to ferry the mail out to his light.

In 1917, his supplies ran out earlier than expected. By Christmas all he had was a little flour and a few limp vegetables. A supply ship trying to land on Kains was twice driven off by heavy seas. One day Sadler spotted a vessel four miles off and rushed for his skiff. He tried three times to push it into the angry waters but was thwarted by ten-foot waves. At last he was able to launch it, only to collide with a floating log. The skiff overturned, pinning him beneath it. When he could finally free himself, he was stunned by a second log. For the next hour he was thrown back and forth by the fury of the water until he managed to stagger up the cliff to the lighthouse.

The spectacle of her husband bruised, dripping wet, and exhausted unnerved Sadler's wife, who seemed unable to speak. She could not sleep that night, imploring him again and again never to take his skiff out into such a sea. At her urging he requested a transfer, but no response came. Every day they watched in vain for a boat while he tried to buoy up her spirits, for she was pregnant with their fourth child.

They saw ship after ship pass by the island until, with his wife and one child ill, he determined to launch the skiff the moment the next steamer appeared on the horizon. The attempt was in vain. Rowing hard, while his wife pumped the hand horn from land, he soon realized that the wind was blotting out the blasts. Exhausted by his fruitless effort, Sadler rowed back and collapsed on the rocks.

In July, relief arrived at last in the form of the government tender *Leebro*. But the captain had received no orders to remove the Sadler family. He went back to his ship, sent off a message inexplicably stating "everything okay," and went on his way. Early in September 1918, a launch anchored off the island and Sadler rowed out to pick up a sack of mail. But there was no letter from the then Department of Marine and Fisheries (later the Department of Transport), only a short notice from "somewhere in France." His wife's younger brother had been killed in action.

With that news, Catherine Sadler's mind snapped. She became so violent her husband had to tie her to the bed. A week passed with the poor woman out of her mind and the children suffering from lack of nourishment. One day Sadler spotted the steamer *Malaspina* nosing through the haze. He sounded the distress signal—four quick blasts on the horn—but the vessel didn't stop. On the eighth day, another ship—a whaler—passed the island. He locked up the children, tied his wife spread-eagled to the bed, and raced for the horn. The ship gave no hint that it had heard or noticed anything. But at the very last moment a seaman with a telescope glimpsed a lone figure lying on the rocks. When they rescued him, Sadler was so far gone he was unable to speak.

His wife was clearly demented. Worry over her children and the family's perilous financial condition had deranged her. After she was committed to the provincial asylum at New Westminster, Sadler left the service.

This case was by no means unusual, as Graham's research has shown. More than one lightkeeper was driven mad by the isolation. Holidays were a luxury that few could afford because, being under contract, the keeper would have to hire a replacement out of his own pocket if he wished to take time off. And with inflation, the helper's wages were sometimes as great as his own.

Yet there were some who endured the lightkeeper's lonely life and actually

More than one lightkeeper was driven mad by the isolation. Holidays were a luxury that few could afford.

thrived in isolation. As Graham has written, "The lights' allure can far outshine life in the real world." Widows carried on after their husbands' deaths; sons took over from fathers. Ben Codville was one of these. He spent over forty-six years on Pointer Island, not far from Bella Bella—the last twenty-nine as his father's replacement. His wife, Annie, was, in effect, a mail-order bride; he married her without leaving his post. His mother, seeing he had no chance to meet a woman, sent off his picture with the mission boat, and Annie fell in love with it. She and Ben were married by the captain of the mission boat that brought Annie from Vancouver.

Ben and Annie Codville

The Codvilles made isolation a passion. Their only contact with the outside world was through newspapers, which arrived in bundles, weeks old. When the couple finally emerged from isolation in 1945, they had never seen a car, a paved road, a cash register, a revolving door, or a telephone, and only rarely other women or children. Their house had been crammed with old newspapers, and when they left they couldn't bear to part with them, so they took them along. They were so used to a wood stove that they refused to switch to oil or gas, nor would they have anything to do with the new-fangled electrical equipment that they had never known during their long exile.

For the wives living on these rocky outposts, life was especially hard. They helped their husbands operate the light but received no pay or benefits. In 1923, a Red Cross nurse, visiting some of the remote lights on B.C.'s Inside Passage, was astonished to find that many of the keepers' wives hadn't set eyes on another woman for as long as fourteen months.

"My wife has gone crazy," William Hartin of Egg Island, north of Queen Charlotte Sound, reported to the department in September 1919. Lack of mail was the main cause of breakdown; in the previous year they had received only four packs of letters.

For any lightkeeper—or his wife—a full night's sleep was out of the question. The light, in order to flash at regular intervals, had to rotate. That was achieved by a set of weight-driven gears, as on a grandfather's clock. Thus, every three hours the keeper (or his wife) had to rouse himself, trudge out to the light, and rewind the machinery, cranking the counterweights up from the floor.

Why, one wonders, would anybody have wanted to take such a job? One reason may have been that the general public had no idea of the sacrifices that were required.

Many lightkeepers arrived at their desolate outposts with no understanding of what the work entailed. But there did seem to be advantages. Though the pay was meagre, it was steady. And the job, a patronage post, required no previous training. Applicants who voted the right way and knew the right people had the inside track. There was something more: the title "lightkeeper" carried a certain cachet.

The death of a lightkeeper presented an appalling problem. On New Year's Day, 1923, Tom Watkins, the keeper of a light perched perilously on a rock in the sea about thirty miles from Prince Rupert, was stricken with pneumonia. His wife took over, spending every waking moment at his bedside or in the lantern room, hoping that some passing vessel might spot her distress signal. None did.

He died after a month, leaving her facing a dreadful dilemma. The department had supplied no shovels since the island was bereft of soil. She and her daughters had only one course: to drag the body up the stairs and onto the roof to freeze. A week later a ship came at last, and a shore party chipped the frozen corpse off the roof and took it and the family to Prince Rupert.

The fury of the wind and the power of the seas were such that many Pacific lighthouses faced demolition by the elements. On Pine Island in 1967, a hundred-knot hurricane ripped a cluster of buildings apart. In the engine room, the very floor on which the lightkeeper and his wife had been standing was laid open to the sky. They spent the night crouched on higher ground around a makeshift fire, pondering the miracle of their survival. Soon after that they quit the service.

Natural disasters—and some man-made ones—were part of every lightkeeper's existence. In 1928, Victoria received a curt but poignant message from Michael O'Brien, the lightkeeper on Entrance Island off Gabriola. "My wife drowned last night," he radioed. "Rush a relief immediately."

The lightkeepers' wives, who worked as unpaid assistants, were subject to the same staggering routine as their husbands. Some found themselves so worn down from the twenty-four-hour-a-day shift they could no longer work—such as Mrs. Jack Hunting, who was hospitalized for exhaustion and was forbidden by her doctors to do any further labour. Hunting could not afford to hire a paid assistant to replace her.

The pay was niggardly and grudging. At one point the lightkeepers were earning less than the exploited native Indian labourers. Nor did the department make any allowance for the increases in the cost of living; by 1919, for example, flour had shot up from $5.75 to $13.00 a sack. A promised raise did not come. Instead, in 1932 the lightkeepers suffered a 10 percent cut. In 1947, in spite of postwar prosperity, their wages were cut again.

The lightkeepers' wives, who worked as unpaid assistants, were subject to the same staggering routine as their husbands. Some found themselves so worn down from the twenty-four-hour-a-day shift they could no longer work.

There were other problems. Though the lightkeepers' children were marooned far from schools, the government refused to pay anything towards their education. The work itself could be highly dangerous. To reduce friction, the mantles and reflectors were floated on a tub filled with mercury. The danger of mercury poisoning was ever present. In the heat of summer the lightkeepers were inhaling mercury "like steam in a sauna."

The more direct dangers were exemplified by Sophie Moran's accident on November 22, 1929. She was wrenched off her feet when the hem of her dress caught in the flywheel of the winch-house. Dragged up against the wheel, she "became a human spoke." Her husband freed her with a kitchen knife, ripping away both flesh and fabric. She suffered dreadfully for a week until the tender *Alberni* picked her up. Her husband found a Workmen's Compensation form, meticulously completed the accident report, and mailed it to the department by the next boat. The claim was rejected because Sophie Moran was working not for the government but for her husband. It was his obligation, as her employer, to compensate her for her injuries.

The government glossed over the problems that the lightkeepers faced. The Morans, for instance, had no way of calling for help because they had no phone. This evidence to the contrary, government spokesmen kept declaring, wrongly, that the majority of keepers were so equipped. There were no paid holidays; in spite of a desperate plea from the lightkeepers' fledgling union, the proposal was turned down. C.D. Howe, then Minister of Transport, intimated that the lightkeepers' lot was similar to that of "a farmer or small merchant," who had no need for time off. Their work, Howe suggested, was really one long holiday, "a family affair."

No doubt Howe's remarks sounded plausible to many couples seeking to escape the fever of city life. The idea of living together on their own patch of ground (or rock) seemed idyllic. One such couple was Laurie Dupuis and his common-law wife, Peggy, whose story is perhaps the most heartrending of all the tales dug up by Donald Graham.

In 1950, Peggy left her husband in Victoria to take up with the handsome lightkeeper on Egg Island, at the entrance to Fitzhugh Sound. She brought her fourteen-year-old son, Stanley, with her, and at first it all seemed an idyllic and romantic adventure. Everything the songwriters, poets, and philosophers had written was true "about the paradise of isolated islands," she wrote in the *Vancouver Sun*. ". . . Just think, no time clock to punch and no bus to catch! If you want to go fishing on a nice day, as soon as routine chores are done, you go."

Soon, however, the isolation began to get on the couple's nerves. She had her man, he had her—and no one else: no friends in whom to confide, no marriage counsellor, not even a handy bar in which to seek solace. As their idyll began to unravel, so did their affection for one another. Tensions grew, accentuated by a dreadful gale in October that wiped out the winch-house and derrick, swept the boathouse into the sea, and wrenched fuel tanks from their footings.

Laurie grew jealous when, on a trip to Port Hardy, other men danced with his woman. On the way back he confided to a radio operator that during one of their spats she had threatened to leave him. Perhaps she was planning to return to her ex-husband! Back at the light, things grew worse. Peggy had to leave for minor surgery in Vancouver and took Stanley with her. Bereft, Laurie tried to patch matters up by writing her a letter a day for eight weeks, underlining his loneliness. These piled up on the table, awaiting her return.

Communication by radiophone was often unclear in those days. The radio operator at Bull Harbour passed a personal message to Laurie that threw him into despair. It was from Peggy's ex-husband: "I must have a picture of you. Received your letter. Junior, Good luck." Laurie was certain that his wife's former husband was responding to a letter from her and that she was preparing to leave him, but actually the message was for her son. The whole meaning had been altered by the accidental rearrangement of a period and a comma. In his despair Laurie wrote out his will and placed it with a note and the flawed message in an envelope. Then he picked up a .22-calibre rifle, walked down to the rocks near the boathouse, and shot himself.

The next day Peggy arrived with Stanley, anxious to be reunited. The telegram with the error in punctuation told her part of the story. So did Laurie's letter: "I would sooner die than live without you." The corpse sprawled over the rocks said the rest.

"Wife of Egg Island Lighthouse Keeper Finds Life of Isolation Fascinating," her article for the Victoria *Colonist* was headlined. But the fascination had been short-lived and the isolation had been too much. Although she went on to apply for her late husband's post, declaring that Egg Island was "the only life"—a remarkable statement, given the history of her exile—she must have thought better of it, for she stayed only until a replacement could be found.

The days of the manned lights are almost over now. By the year 2000, every light on the Pacific coast will have been automated. This change means that the U.S. Department of Defense, through its satellite network, now does the work. For a saving of $3.4 million a year we have handed over control of our navigational safety to a foreign power. The official reason has nothing to do with sovereignty or with tragedy, isolation, loneliness, despair, or disaster. As always, the big changes have been justified not by human compassion, but in the interests of saving money.

The days of the manned lights are almost over now. By the year 2000, every light on the Pacific coast will have been automated.

B.C.'s LOVE AFFAIR WITH THE SEA

On the Pacific coast, the sea provides the greatest recreation. Yachtsmen, kayakers, surfboarders, and rowing crews all make use of it, and some even live on it year-round in gaily painted houseboats.

A holidayer in a kayak drinks in the vistas of the Khutzeymateen Inlet, one of the mountain-encircled fiords north of Prince Rupert.

You can jog for seven miles around the seawall of Vancouver's Stanley Park, a rain forest within a stone's throw of skyscrapers.

Victorians, including this roller-blading teenager, make full use of their ocean front. Washington State lies just across the water.

Cyclists speed across the flat surface of Long Beach in Vancouver Island's Pacific Rim National Park. At right, a rowing crew works out in Vancouver's Coal Harbour. The Pan Pacific Hotel in the background looks like a ship under full sail.

Kim McMillan enjoys a coffee break on the deck of her floating home, one of many anchored off Granville Island in the city's False Creek.

A village of houseboats, each architecturally unique and connected by duckboards, epitomizes Vancouver's love of the water.

In the old days there was no road to Long Beach. You could reach it only by taking a boat to the western coast of Vancouver Island. Today it's a surfer's paradise—and also a playground for kids.

B.C.'s many ferries cater to commuters and tourists alike. This one makes its way up Jervis Inlet from Saltery Bay to Earls Cove.

Every British Columbian seems to own a boat and most go fishing, like this pair not far from Skidegate in the Queen Charlottes.

LAND SCAPES

Along the ever-changing continental shoreline the camera's lens
unveils a rich mosaic of odd configurations.

Cape Burney on the doorstep of the North West Passage

THE ARCTIC COAST

TO VILHJALMUR STEFANSSON, THE FROZEN SEACOAST AT THE TOP OF THE continent was "the friendly Arctic," a phrase that was to provoke a good deal of controversy during the explorer's lifetime and one that continued after his death. Is the Arctic all that friendly? Stefansson's theory was that white North Americans could survive easily in the frozen world if they adopted Inuit customs. The irony is that the Inuit, instead, have begun to adopt the lifestyle of the South. The komatik and the igloo have already been replaced by the snowmobile and the tarpaper shack.

We know very little about the Arctic, and much of what we do know is myth. Yes, it is cold, but not as cold as parts of Northern Ontario where the Arctic record low of minus 63°F has been exceeded. (I have seen the temperature drop to minus 69° in the Peace River country.) Snag, Yukon, five hundred miles south of the Arctic coast, holds the national record for low temperature, a chilling minus 80° F.

And, yes, there is snow, but not as much as the prairies experience. Much of the Arctic is desert, with an average precipitation no greater than that of the Sahara. Several factors make the Arctic forbidding: the extremes of temperature, the unusual length of the seasons (the brief, elusive summers, the long, sunless winters), and the howling gales that can blow the snow off the naked hills and create fifteen-foot drifts at their bases.

There are two Arctics, as Douglas Wilkinson, a seasoned Arctic hand, has pointed out: the spectacular "vertical" Arctic to the east and northeast, all mountains, cliffs, and ice-caps, dominated by the monstrous islands—Baffin, Ellesmere, Devon, and Axel Heiberg—and the western "horizontal" Arctic, a vast area of featureless lowlands, devoid of trees, the soil shallow, the bedrock exposed.

Into this monotonous land, unmarked by roads, fences, railways, or powerlines, a spectral intruder has crept. This is the reddish-brown "Arctic haze," first observed in the 1950s, composed of tiny particles containing a wide variety of contaminants. Each winter prevailing winds carry this tainted cloud from the industrialized cities of Eurasia to the frozen seacoast. We tend to think of the Arctic as being as clean and pure as, well, the driven snow. That is a myth we can no longer cherish.

CHAPTER FOUR

THE ELUSIVE PASSAGE

LONG BEFORE THE MEN OF THE ROYAL NAVY BEGAN TO EXPLORE THE ARCTIC archipelago there was considerable evidence that there was no practical North West Passage to the Orient. Yet the prospect of finding a shortcut that might lead to the silks, spices, and treasures of the mysterious East was so alluring that men of probity clung to it like limpets.

There had once been a time, in Champlain's day or even later, when the possibility of some kind of channel through the midriff of the continent could not be dismissed. Most of North America at that time was unmapped and unexplored. The broad St. Lawrence led to the even broader Great Lakes. China seemed to be just beyond those waters. How much more of North America was there, anyway?

Nobody could be sure, but after that meticulous mariner George Vancouver had done his plotting of every foot of the Pacific coast and found no opening that might be the passage's mouth, the speculation might have ended. It didn't. The wishful thinkers merely moved the probable passage north to the unknown territory of the frozen world, a vast realm that no white man had ever seen.

They believed in the passage because they wanted to, just as many dreamers were infatuated with the myth of the Open Polar Sea. Without a shred of evidence, some, who ought to have known better, conceived of a temperate ocean, free of ice, surrounding the North Pole, and walled off from the world by a frozen barrier. There were even references to a strange race of beings living along its shores. Anyone who believed that would believe in anything, including the prospect of a lane of navigable water linking the two oceans. John Barrow did, and he was the civil servant who persuaded the British Admiralty to outfit naval expeditions to seek this will-o'-the-wisp.

Was it all frozen ocean or was it solid land—a fog-shrouded realm at the top of the world? Nobody knew. In Barrow's day the great Arctic archipelago, with its two thousand islands, was no less mysterious than the cratered moon. Although Samuel Hearne and Alexander Mackenzie had reached the Arctic's rim in the eighteenth century, the seacoast was unmapped and unexplored. For all anybody knew, the continent might easily stretch as far north as the Pole itself.

Except for Henry Hudson's great bay and a chunk of Baffin Island, the Arctic was a blank on the map. Why not a passage? Since the days of that swashbuckling Elizabethan Martin Frobisher, it had captured the imagination of the English.

Unlike most explorers, Robert McClure entered the Passage from the west. His ship, Investigator, became trapped in the ice pack at the northern tip of Banks Island, August 20, 1851.

Frobisher thought he'd found it in a strait he believed led directly to the Pacific, complete with an island of gold at its mouth. But the strait was only a bay, and the treasure turned out to be fool's gold. In 1631, Luke Foxe, back from exploring the channels north of Hudson Bay, put a damper on further speculation when he reported that there could be no passage south of the Arctic Circle. At that, interest began to wane.

Then, nearly two centuries later, this obviously useless and perhaps mythical lane of water suddenly became the prize—the one that every mariner sought with a fixity that bordered on obsession. The great age of exploration was dawning, an age in which explorers were idolized like the rock stars of a later era, when books on Arctic travel were gobbled up by an eager public, when rewards of thousands of pounds were offered to those who could successfully penetrate the Arctic: five thousand pounds to the man who reached a longitude of 110 degrees; ten if he went twenty degrees farther west; fifteen if he attained another thirty; and twenty thousand pounds if he reached the Pacific—a tax-free sum worth more than a million dollars today.

Why all this hullabaloo over a channel of water that was commercially worthless? A good deal of claptrap has been written about the romance of exploration, the spirit of the age, humankind's quest to conquer the unconquerable. Actually, the British officers who left their names on those bleak islands went north cheerfully because they wanted fame, fortune, and promotion; ordinary seamen did so because they were told to.

If Nelson had lost the battle of Trafalgar or Napoleon had remained on the French throne, the search for the passage would have taken a different course. But Britain had won, Britain was cocky, and Britain was burdened with a surfeit of ships and men. Something had to be found for them to do, and John Barrow thought he knew what that something was. Why not pack them off to the seven seas on voyages of exploration for the greater glory of the Empire? The fabled passage was the greatest prize of all; it was Britain's destiny. What a comedown it would be if some other nation discovered it first!

The Victorians kept records obsessively. They charted the seas, mapped every foot of new territory, made thousands of minute observations, meticulously noted and indexed the flora and fauna of each new land, collected geological specimens, and exhaustively studied the habits of aboriginal peoples. But from this mountain of research they learned precious little because they refused to adapt to new environments, preferring instead to bring their own with them. Tight-fitting uniforms of British wool were as unsuitable in the sweltering heat of the South Pacific as they were in the numbing cold of the Arctic. No matter; the stubborn British insisted on clinging to the product of England's dark, satanic mills.

The Royal Navy blundered into the Arctic, blithely unaware that anything was wrong. In fact, *everything* was wrong. The clothing was wrong; the ships were wrong; the food was wrong; the sledges were wrong; their very notion of Arctic travel was wrong. In their myopia and their arrogance, they refused to learn from the whalers, from the fur traders, and, most of all, from the squat, resourceful indigenous people who knew how to survive in the frozen world.

No civilian could tell the Navy anything. They had beaten Napoleon, hadn't they? After that anything was possible. The man best qualified to attempt the first breach of the supposed passage in 1818 was William Scoresby, the most knowledgeable and skilful of the Greenland whalers. But Scoresby wasn't Navy, and he belonged to the wrong social class. It was unthinkable that a member of this despised group should be placed in charge of one of His Majesty's ships. Scoresby offered advice; the Navy snubbed him.

Scoresby knew what the Navy didn't know: the Arctic weather was dangerously fickle. The ice was forever shifting and changing so that a channel might be wide open one year and frozen solid the next. William Edward Parry, the first European to enter the islands, found that out. In a remarkable feat in 1819, Parry got his ships through five hundred miles of ice-free channels as far as Melville Island on the far edge of the archipelago. To his dismay he found he couldn't duplicate that achievement in two subsequent tries. Three decades would pass before anyone did.

By 1827 Parry had given up and turned his attention to the North Pole. Again, he ignored the foremost authority on the geography of the Arctic, the whaler Scoresby, whose monumental book has been called the foundation of Arctic science. Scoresby had sixty thousand miles of experience sailing in Arctic waters. In his book and in earlier lectures he had made several sensible points about Arctic travel. But these were ignored by the British Admiralty right up to the last abortive expedition in 1875–76.

Scoresby had pointed out that the best mode of travel was by light, flexible sledges built on slender wooden frames covered with waterproof skins—the kind the Inuit used. These, he said, should be pulled by dogs and would require trained dog drivers. But the Navy ignored his advice. Parry instead built two cumbersome, seventy-foot-long sledges, each weighing three-quarters of a ton. The beasts of burden would be not dogs, but naval ratings, struggling to the point of exhaustion as they manhandled these behemoths over a rumpled terrain marked by great fissures and pressure ridges.

No civilian could tell the Navy anything. They had beaten Napoleon, hadn't they? After that anything was possible.

Eighty-five years later, the Royal Navy was still ignoring the one practical means of locomotion that the Inuit had perfected over the centuries. As late as 1911 the great Norwegian Fridtjof Nansen was urging Robert Falcon Scott to take dogs on his expedition to the South Pole. You could, Nansen pointed out, eat your dogs in a pinch. Scott was horrified. Eat man's best friend? To an Englishman that was close to cannibalism.

George Nares, on the last of the British naval expeditions to the Arctic in 1875, did take dogs but did not use experienced dog drivers as Scoresby had advised. The canines were treated as playthings. On his sledge journeys, men, not animals, were in the traces, each dragging two hundred pounds of weight over the hummocky ice.

The British preferred to do things the hard way; there seems, indeed, to have been a feeling that the use of animals for transport was a form of cheating. There was something noble, something romantic, about sturdy young men marching in harness through the Arctic wastes, enduring incredible hardships with smiles on their lips and a song in their hearts.

During his famous expedition to search for Sir John Franklin, Leopold M'Clintock gave his sledges names that suggested knightly virtues: Inflexible, Hotspur, Perseverance, Resolute. Each sledge had its own motto, some even in Latin: *Never Despair, Faithful and Firm*. Off they went, fifteen sledges in two long rows, the six-man crews loping across the ice like so many schoolboys, dragging loads of more than a ton with three hearty cheers ringing in their ears. Within a fortnight, M'Clintock had to send a third of them home suffering from exhaustion, rheumatism, and frostbite. A week later, more stumbled back. Small wonder that one Arctic veteran, Captain Henry Kellett, declared that sledge travelling was far more dreadful than battle.

In its arrogance, the Navy referred to M'Clintock as the father of modern sledging. Much was made of his record journeys over the ice. In fact, the Hudson's Bay fur traders, using dogs, snowshoes, and lighter, flexible sledges, had made much longer ones with less stress. But then, in the social hierarchy of the Royal Navy, fur traders didn't count.

The fur traders had learned from the Inuit; the naval explorers had learned nothing. Again, the snobbery of the English class system did them in. The Americans, who followed later, came from a frontier nation that had learned to profit from the experience of the aboriginals. The British stubbornly continued to sweat and then freeze in their leather and wool while the Americans wore furs—boots of dogskin, breeches of sealskin, jumpers of reindeer hide, and caps and masks of oilskin. But the British were terrified of "going native"—in their view the worst and most degrading fate any highborn Englishman could suffer.

The Royal Navy spurned dogs and insisted that its men drag their heavy sledges over some of the roughest terrain in the world.

The Navy even slept in duffel coats and blanket bags, a practice that Dr. John Rae of the Hudson's Bay Company had discarded in the 1840s, adopting instead the Inuit example of individuals sleeping together half naked under a loose covering. The blanket bag, Rae pointed out, separated the men from each other so they could not communicate the heat from one body to another. But Rae was a fur trader, not a naval man.

No one apparently thought to study why the Inuit remained healthy while the white men tottered weakly about with blotched limbs and ulcerated gums—symptoms of the scurvy that ravaged almost every Arctic expedition during its second year. The Navy's favourite antiscorbutic was lemon juice, wrongly referred to as lime juice (hence the derogatory appellation "limey"). No one connected the native diet of raw seal blubber and the half-digested contents of caribou stomachs (both loaded with vitamin C) with their surprising freedom from the disease. Instead, the white explorers looked upon this habit with contemptuous distaste. Parry found it "horrible and disgusting"; Alexander Armstrong, the ship's doctor on the *Investigator* during the search for Franklin, thought the natives were "the most filthy race on the face of the globe." None realized that the benefits of freshly killed meat, eaten raw, in staving off scurvy had been documented by the navy's own John Ross, himself a figure of controversy.

The most celebrated of the Arctic voyages to seek the passage, and, by common-sense standards, the most inept, was John Franklin's abortive quest and the eleven-year search for him that followed. It was almost inevitable that the effort would cost that aging explorer his life and also those of his entire crew.

Franklin was an unlikely choice to lead an Arctic expedition. He was crowding sixty, an advanced age in those times. As a commander he was amiable enough and certainly brave, as his service in the Napoleonic Wars had shown. He was also urged on by a reckless ambition and a hunger for fame and promotion—an appetite that had caused the deaths of eleven of his party during his first land expedition across the barren grounds of northern Canada. He himself was within days of death when he was saved by the fortuitous arrival of an Indian band.

Later, when as governor of Van Diemen's Land he was outmanoeuvred by a canny civil servant, he was shipped home in what he considered a form of disgrace. Nothing would do but that he retrieve his fading honour by leading another expedition, his fourth, into the frozen world. He didn't get the job because of his abilities; he got it because his friends and colleagues in the Navy felt sorry for him.

His expedition would be the largest yet to seek the passage—134 men (later reduced to 129 by sickness) embarking on two barque-rigged sailing ships designed for war and not for the twisting channels of the Arctic. What was the Navy thinking? Coastal ships were what was needed, not bulky craft designed for the open ocean. And so many men! Here was a classic example of overkill. If things went wrong, a ship's crew of that size could not sustain itself on any of the bleak Arctic islands. But almost no one gave so much as a second thought to the possibility of trouble. Only one of Franklin's officers, his second-in-command, Francis Crozier, had any polar background, and Crozier himself was concerned. "Look at the state our commander's ship is in," he told a fellow officer. "Everything in confusion. He is very decided in his own views but has not good judgement."

Franklin had stocked his ships with a 1,200-book library, which contained John Ross's shrewd comment on the need for fresh meat to combat scurvy. But Franklin's officers would not stoop to hunt game. His menus depended heavily on salt meat and on the small birds that the crew shot for sport. Preserved in salt, the birds were useless as antiscorbutics. Franklin expected his crew to live on their own stock of provisions and to keep down scurvy with the classic ounce of lemon juice a day, which was inadequate to protect them.

The cumbersome expedition set sail in the spring of 1845. The two little ships were glimpsed that June by some Greenland whalers and never seen again by Europeans. They were loaded down with mountains of provisions and all the necessities of nineteenth-century naval travel—fine china, silver plate, cut glass, mahogany desks, lead lining for boats, and heavy oak for sledges—much of which would be found years later, broken, tarnished, or rotting, on the cold shores of an unmapped Arctic island.

More than forty expeditions were mounted to search for the elderly explorer. So sure was Franklin of success that he neglected the standard naval practice of leaving cairns in his wake to mark his passage. As a result, ship after ship blundered about the Arctic searching every strait and corner except the right one. In the end it wasn't the British Navy that unearthed the first clues to Franklin's route; it was a private expedition underwritten by the dead explorer's indomitable widow and captained by one of the despised whalers, William Penny. It was he who discovered on Beechey Island the graves of three seamen who had died of tuberculosis in the expedition's first year.

Franklin's two ships were imprisoned forever in the frozen channel west of King William Land. It was here that Leopold M'Clintock found the cairn that contained the only reference to Franklin's own fate ever discovered. He had died of unknown causes in June 1847. Franklin was dead before his crews vacated the ice-bound ships. They built the cairn at Victory Point and struggled across the barren

They were loaded down with mountains of provisions and all the necessities of nineteenth-century naval travel—fine china, silver plate, cut glass, mahogany desks, lead lining for boats, and heavy oak for sledges.

101

island, dying by inches from exhaustion, scurvy, and, as modern research indicates, lead poisoning caused by imperfect soldering of the tins holding preserved meat.

Franklin had determined to follow Victoria Strait off the western coast of King William Land because he thought the land mass was a peninsula, not an island. In his ship's library was a book by the waspish surgeon-naturalist Richard King, who was equally sure that the so-called peninsula was an island that could be circumvented easily by sailing down the eastern side. King was right, as he often was, but he wasn't Navy and his advice was ignored.

The British hankering for losers made a hero out of Franklin. He hadn't reached the passage, but, it was argued, he'd seen it in the distance. Thus ended the long search that, as a by-product, established Great Britain's, and later Canada's, sovereignty over the Arctic.

More than half a century would pass before any ship could successfully make it through the passage, such as it was. In 1903, Roald Amundsen and half a dozen comrades managed it in the little herring boat *Gjöa*. They wore native clothing, slept in snow houses, and over two winters managed to travel from Baffin Bay to Herschel Island off the Yukon coast. It was an adventure that required the kind of meticulous preparation and planning the Royal Navy scorned. Throughout the voyage and before it they listened carefully to the Inuit, who taught them how to dress, how to live in the cold and survive. None of the afflictions visited upon the early explorers—scurvy, exhaustion, starvation, or semi-madness—weakened Amundsen's tight little group of comrades. Indeed, he made it look so easy that history has tended to depreciate him. What he proved was a negative: there was no practical passage in the Arctic by any of the five routes available.

The passage still beckons and the passage still intrigues. Since Amundsen's day there have been about forty complete transits and more than seventeen hundred partial transits. Henry Larsen of the RCMP took the little *St. Roch* through three times—once from the west, twice from the east. Sometimes it seems there is a veritable traffic jam of vessels in those serpentine channels: a Dutch ketch, a Japanese sloop, a Canadian kayak, a French sailing ship, an American motor launch, a Bahamas-registered passenger liner, not to mention research vessels, submarines, icebreakers, and oil tankers. The commercial possibilities have only just been explored. Anyone willing to pay several thousand dollars for the privilege can now make it through the passage, or part of it. One could almost say that the North West Passage, which shattered so many dreams and caused so many tragedies, is now in danger of becoming a tourist trap.

September 6, 1850: the passage beckons beyond Prince of Wales Strait, but Robert McClure cannot force his way through the floating ice.

FIRST VIEWS OF THE PASSAGE

These photographs show the entrance to the North West Passage as it appeared to the first European explorers who ventured past Baffin Island and into the unknown. Little has changed since those days.

The dramatic coast of Baffin Island as Edward Parry saw it when he crossed Baffin Bay to become the first white man to enter the Arctic.

The mountainous east coast of Baffin, the world's fourth-largest island, has scarcely changed since Edward Parry first saw it in 1819.

The island is named for the pilot William Baffin, who first explored it in 1616. It was "lost" for two centuries.

The steep cliffs of Baffin Island, seen from Pond Inlet, bear no relation to the featureless tundra of the Western Arctic's sullen coastline.

Sunset at Nanisivik, an Inuit village off Admiralty Inlet, the world's longest fiord, near the northern tip of Baffin Island.

ABOVE: The early explorers ventured down the ice-choked channel of Admiralty Inlet deep into Baffin's interior, only to find it was not a continuation of the passage but just another dead end.

RIGHT: Floating icebergs proved hazardous as the first Europeans passed Bylot Island off Baffin's northern coast. Westward lay the unknown.

Cape Burney on the east coast of Bylot Island guards the entrance to Lancaster Sound, gateway to the North West Passage.

Sailing west beyond Baffin, the early explorers entered the heart of the Arctic, passing by Devon Island, a vast, barren plateau of frost-shattered rock nearly devoid of plant or animal life.

CHAPTER FIVE

WHAT HAPPENED TO THE WHALES?

T HE WHALING INDUSTRY, AS ITS HISTORIAN, DANIEL FRANCIS, REMINDS US, WAS "in the great tradition of Canadian resource industries—uncontrolled, rapacious, and foreign-owned." In the Canadian Arctic it reached its zenith. There, it attracted more ships, employed more men, and produced greater profits than whaling anywhere else in North America.

Between 1700, when the Dutch first began to search for whales in Davis Strait, and 1915, when whaling was no longer profitable, it was estimated that twenty-eight thousand bowhead whales had been killed in Baffin Bay alone. At the end of the commercial whaling cycle, there were fewer than six hundred left in the Arctic.

Conservation was always a foreign concept to the whalers. Their main preoccupation was to slaughter as many whales as possible, unhampered by any government legislation. Even after Canada gained control of the Arctic archipelago in 1880, nobody gave a hoot about the declining numbers of the bowhead.

The few voices of protest were drowned out in the Arctic gales. As early as 1886, Commander A. R. Gordon predicted the bowhead would become extinct unless a five-year moratorium were established. It wasn't, of course. In 1903, the distinguished Canadian geologist and explorer A. P. Low reported that "the future of the whaling industry appears to be very gloomy. . . . The enterprise is reduced to almost a gambling chance." Few paid any attention. By 1907, Joseph-Elzéar Bernier, after a two-year patrol through the Arctic, reported to the government that "the whaling fishery is exhausted." The fleet had been reduced from 150 ships to a mere 8. Even that was too many. In two summers, Bernier reported, he had sighted only one bowhead whale.

The whale that changed the economy of the Arctic was an eighty-ton monster whose head, the size of a modern living room, occupied one-third of the animal's body. Unlike many other whales, it was slow and easy to pursue; after it was killed its carcass conveniently rose to the surface of the water.

Flensers go to work on a whale with the mother ship close alongside. The baleen in the whale's mouth can be easily spotted.

It was also a floating treasure trove. Instead of teeth, its mouth was filled with curtains of baleen. The elastic horn-like substance in the whale's cavernous mouth acted as a sieve for the plankton on which the animal fed. When heated, baleen became flexible and could be twisted into various shapes. Where would the nineteenth-century fashion industry have been without whalebone corsets? Baleen was the plastic of its day, essential for buggy whips, skirt hoops, umbrellas, carriage

wheels and springs, luggage, and fishing rods. Even the fringe hairs were used to manufacture brushes and stuff furniture.

Before the refinement of petroleum, oil from whale blubber was the standard lubricant for machinery. Before electricity, major British cities fuelled their street lighting systems with it. The British wool industry required large quantities to clean wool before spinning it. In the eighteenth century, the British needed the whaling industry badly enough to subsidize it. By 1749 the government was paying a bounty of forty shillings a ton to every whaling ship weighing over two hundred tons.

As a result, the British began to replace the Dutch as the major force in Davis Strait whaling, sending as many as one hundred ships a year into the frigid, fog-cloaked waters west of Greenland. Until 1817, however, nobody dared to cross to the Canadian side. The only possible route was to sail up the Greenland coast to the very top of Baffin Bay and navigate around the top of the ice pack to the open water on the far side. In 1817, two British ships did just that, turning up in Lancaster Sound, an unexplored passage at the tip of Baffin Island.

That seemed to break the spell. The following August the first of the Royal Navy's post-Napoleonic exploring expeditions also reached the mouth of the sound, which its commander, John Ross, thought to be a dead end. It wasn't. It led directly into the heart of the Arctic archipelago and would be the route that scores of ships would follow in the years to come.

The Inuit have retained the story of that first encounter with the whalers. The first to see a white man told his friends, "Today I saw something with long legs and long arms I never saw before." He did not realize that this white creature was a fellow member of the human species. "Over there in Pond Inlet," one woman told modern writer Dorothy Harley Eber, "when the first ship was approaching, the people were terrified. They had the shamans then, and went into trances and chanted. The Inuit thought the people on the ship had come to murder them."

The hazardous route from Greenland to Lancaster Sound led off from Melville Bay, a great bite in the big island's west coast. The sailors called it the Breaking-Up-Yard because it claimed more ships than the rest of the Arctic combined. Here, vessel after vessel was smashed to bits by the battering rams of the shifting ice and the capricious winds that howled across the waters. We have one description from a twenty-one-year-old medical student, William Eden Cass, who shipped aboard the whaler *Brunswick* in March 1824.

"It is probable," Cass wrote, "that the most terrific and sublime spectacle in nature is the concussion of these enormous fields and floes. It would indeed be difficult for the human imagination to conceive anything more awful and impressive. . . than when the still and utter silence which had reigned around is suddenly and fearfully interrupted by the meeting of two enormous fields or floes revolving in opposite directions and advancing against each other at the rate of several miles an hour. The one is broken and destroyed or forced in part above the other with a loud and terrible dissonance, resembling the voice of thunder. . . During this terrible contact huge masses of ice are raised with tremendous force above the surface of the water. . . These disruptive masses are . . . very common in Davis Strait, being thrown up to the height of twenty feet from the surface of the field, extending fifty or sixty yards in length and forming a mass of about 2,000 tons in weight."

The worst of many disasters in the Breaking-Up-Yard occurred in 1830 when nineteen ships were sunk—one-fifth of the entire whaling fleet. Twelve more were damaged and twenty-one returned to port without a single whale.

In spite of those losses, the fleet continued to expand as more and more "blubber ships," as they were called ("ungainly snuffboxes" in another description), were turned out by the British shipyards. More than thirty yards long, between 180 and 360 tons, double-planked and fortified with oak and iron, broad of beam to carry an eighty-ton whale alongside, they were tough enough to absorb a collision with the ice and so rugged that a few men could handle them when most of the crew was off in hot pursuit. It was a richly profitable industry, for the whales seemed limitless. In one decade, 1825–34, the catch exceeded 8,500 animals.

For the whalers it was also a hazardous business. A blow from a harpooned whale lashing about in the water could smash a boat to pieces. Whaleboat crews, dragged across miles of ocean by wounded animals, could sometimes lose their bearings in the fog and vanish forever. Others were forced to row for miles with their catch in order to return to their ship.

When the whale's carcass was brought alongside, the bloody process known as flensing began. A harpooner hacked at the dead animal's spinal column with an axe so that the head could be hoisted onto the deck. Then all the harpooners, wearing spurs on their boots and armed with sharp, long-handled spades, jumped onto the floating carcass to remove the blubber, which was chopped into pieces and swung onto the deck. Finally, the kreng, a bloody mass of bones and entrails, was all that was left. By this time, the decks were grimy with blood and oil, so slippery that sawdust had to be dumped onto the work areas until the tramping of the whalers' boots carried it throughout the ship. At season's height the ocean was the colour of

The harpooners, wearing spurs on their boots and armed with sharp, long-handled spades, jumped onto the floating carcass to remove the blubber.

blood and the flensed bodies of scores of whales could be seen along the ice, slowly putrefying and giving off an intolerable stench.

The whalers spent more time in the frozen world than they did at home with their families. The carefree joys of summer were denied them. During twenty-one years of Arctic cruising, the captain of the *Thomas* regretted that he had never been able to taste a strawberry. Another captain, William Barron, recalled, "I never saw either blossom or fruit upon the trees, and my eyes and senses were never blessed with the scent of growing flowers, the sight of ripening corn or the subsequent harvest operations."

There were worse hazards. Caught in the vicelike grip of the ice, the ship was at the mercy of wind and current. A typical example recorded by Daniel Francis was the ill-fated voyage of the *Diana*, one of nine ships trapped in Pond Inlet early in July 1866. The ice did not release the vessels. Having abandoned whaling, the crews began to pick their way south, desperately seeking open water. All but the slower *Diana* made it. By September 22 *Diana* was almost out of coal and short of provisions. The ice pack, in the words of the ship's surgeon, was "heavy . . . beyond the experience of any men in the fleet."

The captain had two options: to winter at Pond Inlet or to stay in the midst of the pack and hope the drift would take *Diana* into the open Atlantic before his crew starved or froze to death. He chose to drift with the current, put his crew on short rations, and used every available scrap of fuel, from barrel staves to upper masts and yardarms.

At the end of November, with the wine freezing in the bottles and a thick coating of ice forming on the walls, *Diana* was carried into Frobisher Bay where she was tossed about for three months before making her escape. In December, when gale-force winds piled the ice deck-high against the hull, the crew abandoned ship, only to return when the winds abated. *Diana* began to take on water; the crew exhausted themselves on the pumps; the captain died of cold and anxiety. The clamour around them seemed unearthly as boards popped with the frost and the frozen rigging rattled in the wind. "We seem to be dwelling in some haunted house filled with unearthly and mysterious noises," one officer wrote.

The first signs of scurvy—the bleeding gums, loose teeth, and bruised limbs—appeared in January. The following month a crewman died. By the end of February most of the sailors had the disease. On March 7, the pack broke up at last and *Diana* steamed clear. Her crew had been imprisoned in the ice for 175 days.

Their ordeal was not over. They still had to survive the journey to England,

The famous steam whaler Maud, *with all sails set, tries to bull her way through the dense ice pack in Davis Strait. The year is 1889.*

but the last of the blubber had been used up. Nothing remained with which to build a fire. The sick men lay in bunks awash with water from the ice melting on the walls. Only a handful had strength enough to carry out their duties. By the time *Diana* reached the Shetland Islands, eight men were dead, their corpses wrapped in canvas and laid out on the deck. Three more died within a few days. In that dreadful whaling season, *Diana* had lost a quarter of her crew and didn't have a cargo to show for it.

For green seamen, unused to Arctic conditions, the harsh life aboard a whaler was sometimes too much. There was more than one case of desertion from an Arctic whaler by men who had no knowledge of their whereabouts and who tried to escape by walking one thousand miles or more with neither chart nor sextant.

On August 4, 1860, nine crewmen left a group of vessels in Cumberland Sound and attempted to reach civilization by whaleboat. By September 3, when they reached the Labrador coast, all their food was gone and two of their number had decamped with all their equipment. When another man died of starvation, his comrades cooked and ate him.

Ravenous the group tried to dispatch a second man, but he fought them off with a pocketknife, mortally wounding one of his assailants. When the wounded man died, the rest ate him, too. The survivors lived on berries, supplementing that diet with their own boots, belts, sheaths, and fragments of bear and sealskin until they were rescued by a group of Inuit without whose help all would have perished.

The arrival of the American whalers in mid-century brought a new relationship with the natives. Not only were the Inuit introduced to a world beyond the Arctic, with new kinds of food and equipment, but they also became participants in the hunt itself. In 1851, Sydney Buddington, first mate of the whaler *McLellan*, volunteered along with eleven companions to spend the winter in an Inuit encampment at Cumberland Sound. The experiment was a success. By being on hand early in the summer, Buddington was able to capture seventeen whales that he could not have harvested had he been forced to return at a later date.

As a result, ship captains began to hire Inuit crews to work for them and supply them with food, blubber, and whalebone in return for the white man's goods. Thus the more entrepreneurial Inuit became partners with the white whalers. This marked a profound change in the economics of the Arctic. Inuit families began to move closer to the winter harbours, becoming less nomadic and more dependent on the white man's goods.

The other side of the coin of prosperity was the simultaneous arrival of the white man's diseases—measles, smallpox, tuberculosis, syphilis, influenza—against which the natives had no immunity. Settlement after settlement was ravaged. The most tragic story of all was the extinction of the Sadlimiut, a stone-age people living on Southampton Island in Hudson Bay. Until the white man arrived at the turn of the century, these primitive people had had almost no contact with white civilization. Even other Inuit groups knew little about the Sadlimiut, who are thought to be the last survivors of the early Dorset culture. They lived in stone houses rather than skin tents and igloos and were using tools made of stone when the whalers arrived. In 1902 disease wiped them out save one woman and four children.

By this time, too, the whales were vanishing from the Eastern Arctic. They didn't swim away; they were simply butchered. The age of steam had arrived, making whaling ships much more efficient. The new harpoon guns and the establishment of winter stations had contributed to the scarcity of sea animals in the area of Davis Strait, Baffin Bay, and Hudson Bay. If the industry were to survive, it would need to find new whaling fields.

One of these appeared in 1888. Charlie Brower, who managed the shore station at Point Barrow, Alaska, heard of a new ground not far from the Mackenzie Delta where whales were said to be "thick as bees." To this point whalers had shunned the shallow waters and dangerous reefs of the Beaufort Sea. With good reason the seamen called it the Forbidden Sea. Just approaching it was hazardous. In August of 1871, the entire fleet of thirty-four whaling ships had been caught in the vicinity of Icy Cape on Alaska's northwest coast. Twenty-seven were destroyed. Five years later, near Point Barrow, fifteen ships trapped in the pack were all lost or destroyed. Few dared to test the waters to the east.

But when Brower's scouts reported that the mighty bowhead was to be found in quantity east of Barrow, the rush for profits was on. By the winter of 1894–95 no fewer than fifteen vessels had made their way to Pauline Cove on Herschel Island at the northern tip of Yukon Territory.

Daniel Francis has given us a lively description of Pauline Cove at its height— a northern boom town straight out of the Old West, crammed with men of every race: "American blacks, Portuguese from the Cape Verde Islands and the Azores, Maoris from New Zealand, 'Kanakas' from the Hawaiian Islands, natives from the Siberian coast, and down-on-their-luck labouring men from the back alleys of San Francisco who had never set foot on a sailing ship before, and probably never would again." This polyglot multitude was cooped up for the nine months of winter with nothing to do but carouse, quarrel, and chase the native women. Many of the ships' officers were brutal and depraved. Boredom and liquor fuelled the

The whales were vanishing from the Eastern Arctic. They didn't swim away; they were simply butchered. The age of steam had arrived, making whaling ships much more efficient.

violence that erupted in this, the last reach of the whaling frontier. As one mission-ary wrote, "The scenes of riotous drunkenness and lust which this island has witnessed, have probably rarely been surpassed."

In 1893 a young missionary who would rise to become a leading Anglican churchman in Canada arrived at Pauline Cove. Isaac O. Stringer, future Archbishop of Rupert's Land, was appalled by the amount of hard liquor being consumed in the community. He persuaded the whaling captains to agree to suspend the liquor traffic, but with limited success. Drunken fights, even murders, were common occurrences. In the end, the rowdiness was curbed because business declined. The whales were harder to come by as more and more whalers were travelling great distances in search of fewer and fewer animals. By 1910, whaling had ceased in the Western Arctic.

In the East the decline continued. In the old days, when whales were plentiful and ship after ship headed for home loaded with baleen, blubber, and oil, the indus-try could absorb major losses resulting from shipwrecks. But by the end of the century the game was no longer worth the candle. Women had stopped using whalebone in their corsets. The new automobiles didn't require whale oil for lubri-cation. There had been a time when a single ship could slaughter as many as forty whales in a season without giving a thought to the future. Now the future had arrived, and it was becoming clear that soon there would be nothing left to kill.

By 1915, with fewer than six hundred bowheads left in the Arctic it was time, belatedly, to call a halt. The hunt ended officially and it became illegal to kill a bowhead. It had taken only two hundred years to destroy the rest.

The future of whaling lies with the native people whose cultural identity has been threatened by the end of an institution central to their lives that goes back to the early days of the Thule people. With the new territory of Nunavut about to become a reality, the Inuit are trying to rebuild some measure of their eroding self-confidence. A return to some form of the traditional Inuit whale hunt is part of the process.

Thanks largely to the work of the newly established Nunavut Wildlife Manage-ment Board, a hunt of sorts has been reinstated. Since 1979 no one had been able to hunt a bowhead whale without a licence. In 1996 it became possible to get a licence to hunt one bowhead a year. In Repulse Bay in 1996, with newspaper writers and TV cameramen in attendance, thirteen selected hunters from ten Inuit communi-ties launched the new whale hunt. It was a long way from the carefree days when dozens of ships emerged from the Arctic fog, loaded with tons of blubber. Even more important than this token reminder of a vanishing culture was the launching by the Wildlife Management Board of a five-year "traditional knowledge study." By the summer of 1997 the bowhead study committee had already travelled to ten native communities, interviewed more than 180 people, mostly elders, and transcribed hours of tape about the bowheads and whaling practices.

It was a subtle admission that for the last two hundred years white men and natives alike had been presiding over the near-extermination of a remarkable sea mammal without really knowing very much about its use by and value to a unique cultural group.

Isaac O. Stringer and his missionary wife pose in native costume after their arrival on Herschel Island in 1883. He rose to become Archbishop of Rupert's Land.

THE DAYS OF
THE WHALERS

Life aboard a whaling ship was hard and often
dangerous. Entire vessels were lost in the ice. But the
real victims were the behemoths of the sea.

ABOVE: A portable crow's-nest sits
on the deck of the whaler Maud
in 1889, just before being hauled
aloft. That's Captain W. Adams
with the telescope.

LEFT: A whaling vessel fights
its way through the icebergs.

*Two whalers scale
the mountainous
corpse of their
quarry to cut away
the oil-rich blubber.*

ABOVE: Photographed during the 1889 whaling season, these gigantic flukes give some idea of the size of the bowhead.

RIGHT: After a kill, the decks of the whaling ships were slippery with blood, grease, oil, and blubber.

FAR LEFT: *A harpooners' boat crew, August 1889.*

ABOVE: *Baleen from the bowhead's cavernous mouth.*

LEFT: *After the baleen was removed, the dead animal's jaw was scrubbed clean of grease and dirt, as photographed in 1912 in the Western Arctic aboard the American whaler* Belvedere.

After the whalers arrived in the Arctic, Inuit hunters quickly absorbed the new techniques and became partners with the white men in the hunt. The photograph at right was taken by Walter Livingstone-Learmonth, who shipped aboard the Maud *in 1889 technically as purser but actually as a paid passenger. His diary of the journey enriches the history of the period.*

FAR LEFT: At New Bedford, Massachusetts, one of the world's leading whaling ports in the 1870s, thousands of casks line the dockside waiting to be loaded and taken north to be filled with whale oil.

LEFT: Like gigantic celery stalks, a cargo of baleen for corsets and buggy whips is delivered to the New Bedford dockside in the 1860s.

CHAPTER SIX

THE CLASH OF CULTURES

I N THE AUTUMN OF 1839, AN ABERDEEN WHALING MASTER, WILLIAM PENNY, brought home a young Inuk named Eenoolooapik ("Eeno" for short). Shortly after his arrival in Scotland, Eeno was invited to a dinner party given expressly to discover how he would conduct himself in Aberdeen society. The surgeon Alexander M'Donald reported that "so far from being in the slightest degree confused, he acquitted himself in a manner that greatly surprised everyone present."

Just one month before, Eeno, in furs and mukluks, had been living among his people in the savage environment of Durban Island at the eastern extremity of Baffin Island. Now, dressed in a fashionable suit, complete with waistcoat and wing-collar shirt, he adapted to this strange environment with astonishing ease, taking note of how his fellow diners acted and copying them with "promptitude and precision." "The smile, the bow, and even the slightest gesture," M'Donald reported, "he imitated with the most minute correctness."

One of the guests at dinner, in order to test him, "purposely committed a breach of etiquette and was immediately followed to the very letter in his unusual course by Eenoolooapik. But being made aware of his error . . . without allowing his self-possession to be at all disturbed, he looked around . . . and readily concluded who he ought to imitate."

Over the centuries, Eeno's people had learned to adjust to a bizarre environment. The Inuit's uncanny powers of observation had been honed in a featureless land where the slightest indentation in a snow-swept plain was enough to serve as a guidepost to home.

Of all the aboriginal people in the New World, the Inuit were surely the most resourceful and adaptable. Consider their attitude to cold. To the white explorers who invaded the Arctic from the Elizabethan era to our own time, snow was an implacable enemy. But long before the white man arrived, the Inuit had learned to use it to keep warm. In the deep freeze of winter, the hard-packed snow of the Arctic became a building material that could be fashioned into blocks with a bone knife. Because it was full of tiny air pockets, it made ideal insulation.

Consider the snow house, a frozen dome constructed of a spiral of blocks, each a different shape from its neighbour. Without using any means of measurement save his eyes and his experience, an Inuk could build one in about an hour, carving and fitting each piece into place like the pieces of an ivory puzzle.

A group of Iwilic natives in a stone house at Cape Fullerton, N.W.T., March 10, 1905.

Or consider the komatik, the Inuit's sole means of transportation until the invention of the snowmobile. Here was an ingenious piece of equipment, the wooden runners braced with lengths of caribou antler fastened by thongs of sealskin, shod with a mixture of pulverized moss and water, and glazed with a thin skin of ice. It was a flexible form of transportation stable enough to speed across the rumpled sea ice without tipping.

An anthropologist, Otto Geist, once made a list of the items the Inuit made from walrus ivory. These included a dog harness buckle, a wound pin to keep a seal from bleeding, part of a fox trap, and a tent line tightener. The list ran to more than one hundred items.

The impact of European culture on these Arctic peoples was inevitable but scarcely beneficial. William Edward Parry, the first white explorer to penetrate the Arctic archipelago, later found that the Christianized Inuit of Hudson Strait had become thieves, pickpockets, and pilferers, so greedy that one even offered to sell her children for trade goods. On the other hand, the natives of Southampton Island and the Melville Peninsula, who had had no contact with whites and thus had no understanding of private property, were honest to a fault. Sledges could be left unguarded without fear of loss. Parry's naval colleague, George Francis Lyon, purposely left, as an experiment, a stock of knives, scissors, looking-glasses, and other objects in a native hut. He wandered off, leaving a dozen Inuit behind, to discover on his return that all his possessions were intact and carefully covered with a skin.

It is not always possible to ascribe generalized characteristics to every Inuk, for even after the white man arrived, many communities were cut off entirely from the world and did not realize that beings like themselves existed elsewhere. Robert McClure, during the Franklin search in the mid-nineteenth century, discovered one such band living on the shores of Prince Albert Land on Victoria Island in the Western Arctic. These people thought they were all alone in the world and were astonished to learn that there were other lands inhabited by human beings.

Their concept of private property differed from the Inuit norm, as McClure learned when he took off a thick red shawl and wound it round the neck of a young woman standing nearby with a child on her back. The practice of unreciprocated gift-giving (which some whites confused with theft) was foreign to this Inuit band; their code required them to offer something of equal value in return. Having nothing else to give McClure, she responded by taking the baby out from under her hood. Covering it with kisses, she proffered it to the embarrassed explorer. Only when it was made clear that he was not proposing barter did she laugh and accept the shawl, which she had refused to touch until this point. What animal was it that had a red skin? she asked. The usually crusty McClure was so moved that he could not refrain from tears as he took his leave.

These natives had an astonishing knowledge of Arctic geography. When McClure supplied one woman with paper she responded by drawing an almost perfect chart, including the coastline. She was able to help the explorer fill in the blanks on his map, making it clear, for instance, that Wollaston "Island" was not insular as everybody had believed.

This ability to remember and use small details and to absorb the lay of the land down to the last wrinkle was remarked on by more than one white visitor. It fits in today with an Inuk's uncanny mechanical ability to take an outboard engine apart and then reassemble it to the last nut. Is it because these resourceful people have instantly memorized the mechanical sequence? Is it because their minds have not been cluttered by extraneous diversions? Their oral tradition suggests both of these possibilities. Certainly the folk memories of the Franklin expedition's last days on King William Island, handed down from one generation to another, exemplify that. A more astonishing example was Charles Francis Hall's discovery of the Frobisher expedition's original landfall, prompted entirely by similar folk memories. In 1861, when the Inuit led Hall to the head of Frobisher Bay and pointed out piles of old coal left from Elizabethan times, foundations of lime and sand, ditches, large pieces of iron and tile, the relics were almost three centuries old. Recollections of Frobisher's expeditions had survived orally for nine generations, the details confirming statements in Frobisher's own account that had been in doubt for years.

The Elizabethan's arrival had coincided with the beginnings of the modern period of Inuit occupation and with the gradual decline of what is known as Thule culture. The native occupation of the Canadian Arctic is only about four thousand

An Inuit hunter in traditional homemade goggles. Modern Inuit prefer shades.

years old, a mere blink in archaeological time. When the so-called Paleoeskimos arrived from Asia about 2000 B.C., the igloo had not yet been devised; these early hunters lived in skin tents and warmed themselves over primitive fires of fat and fatty bones.

Out of this existence grew the Dorset culture. Remnants of Dorset encampments have been found from the Mackenzie Delta to Baffin Island. The Dorset developed the snow house and carved small shamanistic figures of great delicacy from bone and ivory. They were perfectly adaptable to the changing Arctic environment. When the temperature cooled and the herds of musk oxen and caribou dwindled, they moved from the interior to the seacoast to hunt small sea mammals.

Between 900 and 1000 A.D. the weather grew warmer —the same warm period that allowed the Norse to populate Greenland and Iceland. A new, more vigorous, and highly skilled whale-hunting culture we have named the Thule displaced the Dorset. These newcomers were better equipped to hunt the larger whales, and with their dogs and long sledges were also highly mobile.

They spread with comparative speed along the coast from Alaska to Greenland in a few generations. By the sixteenth century, when the Elizabethan explorers first encountered them, a new cooling period had set in, culminating in the Little Ice Age (1650 to 1850 A.D.), when the temperatures were even harsher than they are today, when whales were no longer present in large numbers, when the islands of the High Arctic were deserted, and the old ways of hunting in open water had to be abandoned. The change in the weather, together with the arrival of the Europeans, contributed to the end of the Thule cycle and the beginning of the modern period.

Robert Flaherty, the film-maker (Nanook of the North), *made this study of Nyla, an Inuit mother, and her child at Cape Dufferin off northwestern Ungava.*

In the clash of cultures that followed, the white Europeans and the Inuit each thought theirs was superior. All over the world the English looked down on the native races. But the Inuit were convinced that the Kabloona, as they called them, were distinctly inferior. As Parry noted, "They certainly look upon us in many respects with profound contempt, maintaining the idea of self sufficiency which has induced them . . . to call themselves *Innuee*, or mankind." In his journal, Parry recorded a telling anecdote of an Inuk, Okotook, trying to fasten some gear on a sledge with a white cord. When it broke in his hands, he gave a contemptuous sneer and spat out the expletive: *"Kabloona!"* To him, the material was clearly inferior, but then, what could be expected from a Kabloona?

To the Inuit, the white men were dolts. To the explorers, the Inuit were unwashed savages, "disgusting brutes," in the words of John Ross. They rarely washed because they knew the value of retaining bodily oils in a cold climate. They ate voraciously because they didn't know where their next meal was coming from. The English officers were amused by the enormous quantities of liquids they consumed aboard ship, forgetting that in the Arctic it is foolish to eat snow and thus suffer a perilous loss of body heat. Besides, they could not afford the fuel to melt it, and they were always thirsty. Parry once offered a young Inuk as much food and liquid as he could consume overnight. To everyone's astonishment, he tucked away ten and a quarter pounds of bread and meat and almost two gallons of liquids, including soup and raw spirits.

The natives were as repelled by the white man's diet as the white man was by raw seal liver, whale skin, and blubber. Even the children couldn't stand sweets. The adults spat out rum, refused cups of coffee, and treated a plate of gingerbread as if it were medicine. One woman, who had been left to starve after her husband's death, was offered bread, jelly, and biscuits. She could not stomach any of them and threw them away when she thought nobody was looking.

The straitlaced whites were shocked by the Inuit's "utter disregard for connubial fidelity." But the natives were equally confused and baffled because the English had not brought their wives with them. Every man, they believed, should have at least one wife. Nor could they figure out the British class system. In their society, every man was equal.

The level of misunderstanding between the two cultures was astonishing. The white Europeans despised the Inuit as lazy and slothful. For "slothful" read "patient": patience is the one quality needed for Arctic survival. To sit motionless beside a seal's breathing hole, hour upon hour, until one's dinner pokes its nose above the ice requires a discipline rarely seen among the contestants in the white man's rat race. The white explorers, recklessly eager to achieve new records in mileage travelled, thought of the natives as lazy. But the Inuit knew the value of maintaining a proper pace. In the Arctic, sweat can kill. To overtax one's strength can be fatal because the body is left with no resources to cope with an emergency.

To the Inuit, the white men were dolts. To the explorers, the Inuit were unwashed savages, "disgusting brutes," in the words of John Ross.

Leopold M'Clintock's method of sledging left his men crippled and exhausted for no other reason than vanity. The Inuit arrived at their destinations more slowly but with minds and bodies unimpaired.

The Inuit had no written history and so we do not know of their leaders, criminals, heroes, or even storytellers. In the whole of the Arctic story only a few can be identified by name. We know that four Inuit stood with Robert Peary at the top of the world, but apart from their names—Egingwah, Seeglo, Ooyah, and Ooquah—we know virtually nothing about them. Nor do we know anything further about the two young natives—Ahwelahtea and Etukishook—who Frederick Cook claimed had accompanied him to the Pole, even though Etukishook saved the party's lives when he discovered an old seal carcass his father had cached at Cape Sabine.

We know a good deal more about Minnik, one of six Inuit that Peary brought to New York as trophies on the suggestion of Dr. Franz Boas, assistant curator of the American Museum of Natural History. This is a bitter tale of broken promises and neglect. As Minnik later said, "They promised us nice warm houses in the sunshine land and guns and knives and needles and many other things." These promises were broken. The six natives were housed in the basement of the museum, where they developed colds that turned into pneumonia. They arrived in the fall of 1897; by May 1898, four were dead. One was Minnik's father.

The survivors had difficulty getting back to the Arctic. The youngest, Usaakassak, managed it, but it took Minnik several years, by which time he found it impossible to go back to the old life. He returned to the United States in 1916 and died of influenza two years later. His father's bones were by then part of the museum's collection, but the scientists had kept that knowledge from him by staging a fake funeral, using a log for a corpse.

The brief glimpses we have into the character of a few historical Inuit are blurred because the tale is always told from the white point of view. We get, for instance, a fleeting glimpse of Koojeese, the leading native during Hall's exploration of Frobisher Bay. But Hall was subject to what he would have called Koojeese's "whim." The Inuit leader had no desire to examine every cove and inlet. "You stop; I go," he said peremptorily. Hall was mortified at "being obliged to yield to these untamed children of the north."

We have a more rounded picture of Hall's two guides, Ebierbing ("Joe") and Tookolito ("Hannah"), his constant companions to his death. This pair contradicts the general attitude of the time that the Inuit were generally unemotional—childlike people, always smiling, somewhat like the stereotyped blacks of the American

South. But Tookolito displayed the same range of emotions as any white woman. We see her overcome with joy when she learns that Hall, who had been given up for dead, is very much alive. The tears course down her cheeks and her hands tremble as she embraces him. We see her again when she loses her firstborn. Overwhelmed, she remains unconscious for days to awaken at last, crying piteously but vainly for her lost baby.

She and her husband had acquired a thin veneer of civilization when Hall brought them to England, learning the language and adopting such customs as serving tea. But when her second baby died, the inconsolable mother reverted to the rituals of her people, clinging to the small corpse and walking to the graveside with the tiny body dangling from a loop around her neck as the local *angeko* (shaman) insisted.

White man's grub wasn't always to the Inuits' liking in the early days. But Mr. Christie's biscuits soon became a staple.

Ebierbing and Tookolito were among the ill-assorted group—nine white men, one black cook, four adult Inuit, and five children—who made an incredible voyage that has no parallel in Arctic history. For six months in the winter of 1872–73, they drifted for two hundred miles on windswept ice floes from the top of Baffin Bay to the coast of Labrador. Although a group of German sailors in the party attempted to kill and eat the Inuit, they actually owed their lives to the natives. Ebierbing did most of the hunting for game, while his wife managed to cook two meals a day for them all. Ebierbing went out every day in all temperatures, but the men whose lives were being sustained begrudged him his share of the rations.

George Tyson, the nominal leader of the entire group, wrote an account of the drift for the New York press but didn't devote a word to Ebierbing or any of the other natives. Nor did he have anything to say about Hans Hendrik, another Inuk who helped Ebierbing and who had already played a prominent part in two previous Arctic expeditions. They were shadowy, nameless figures—part of the background, like the icebergs.

The golden age of exploration coincided with the waning of the Thule culture, the emergence of the modern Inuit, and the adoption of white rule in the Arctic. The universal attitude was that the Inuit could only benefit by being turned into ersatz whites. Even Hall, who was closer to the natives than any other explorer, could not rid himself of the mindset of his culture. "The Esquimaux," he wrote, "really deserve the attention of the philanthropist and Christian. Plant among them a colony of men and women having right-minded principles and after some patient toil, glorious fruits will follow."

But it was the right-minded Christians who helped destroy the native culture, even banning the use of the Inuit language in the church and residential schools.

By the 1940s most Inuit had been "civilized." Over the next four decades, in the words of R. Quinn Duffy, they sank "as low as any people could in dirt, degradation, disease, and dependence." The whaling days that had at least given them economic independence were over. The skins of the seals that were part of their way of life as well as the root of their economy were bringing rock-bottom prices because of the animal rights activists, who cared more about animals than people and who knew nothing about the Arctic. The Inuit culture was shattered. They lived in overcrowded shacks, watched TV, and drank heavily.

Yet, as Duffy has also written, "they are the Canadian survivors par excellence." A change of attitude was on the way, sparked by the postwar generation of younger Inuit. James Houston's espousal of Inuit sculpture and print making was certainly a factor: it gave the Inuit artists an economic base as well as a sense of pride. Carving had always belonged to the basic pattern of Inuit life. Now the success of their sculptures led to the establishment of various Inuit co-operatives. By the 1960s these co-ops, taken together, had become the largest single employer in the North.

It quickly became obvious to many natives that they must speak with a united voice. Thus the Inuit Tapirisat was founded to speak for the people, to preserve their heritage, culture, and language, to give them a sense of pride in their heritage, and to help them to achieve full participation in Canadian society.

Coincident with this was the land claims struggle in both the Western and the Eastern Arctic. The most remarkable step forward has been the carving out of a new territorial division, Nunavut (Our Land), twice the size of British Columbia and home to some seventeen thousand Inuit. Stretching from the Manitoba border to the tip of Ellesmere Island, it has been achieved only after a lifetime of negotiation. But when it becomes a reality in April 1999, the Inuit of the Eastern Arctic will at last be in control of their own destinies.

Once again, these resilient people are adapting to new circumstances as they always have. In spite of blue jeans and nylon parkas, snowmobiles and country music, they have not been smothered by the white presence, although they still have a long way to go; joblessness, alcohol, suicide, and despair have not been eradicated in the Arctic communities.

Yet the significance of Nunavut cannot be overestimated. We are witnessing a political revolution in the Arctic. I suspect that it will change Inuit society as profoundly as the Thule culture transformed the Dorset. The difference here is that the change can be measured in decades, not centuries. Anyone who has studied the history of this adaptable people cannot fail to understand that in the face of radical change, they will, as always, prevail and survive.

By 1951, soup mix and shredded wheat, brought by the Eastern Arctic patrol vessel C.D. Howe *to Pond Inlet, had become daily fare.*

DELTA COUNTRY

As the Mackenzie River reaches the Arctic coastline, it splits into dozens of channels to form a bewildering labyrinth of water and muskeg covering 1,500 square miles. Here the muskrats breed by the millions to support, in good times, fur-trading towns such as Aklavik.

The ever-changing Mackenzie Delta as it looked at sunset when André Gallant photographed it from the air in the summer of 1997.

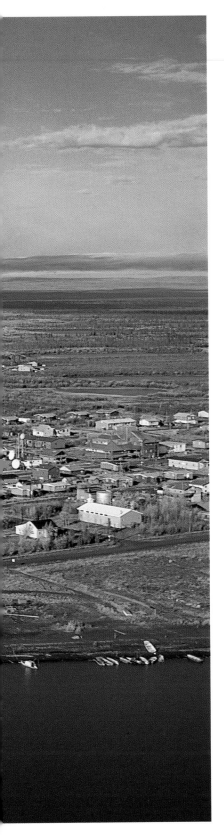

FAR LEFT: Not far from the Mackenzie's mouth, a sandspit pokes its slender finger out into the cold Arctic. Here is the Inuit settlement of Tuktoyaktuk, which means "looks like caribou." Once a whale-hunting settlement, now it's a base for oil and gas exploration.

ABOVE: Two Inuit children pick cranberries in the tundra country not far from Tuktoyaktuk.

LEFT: An Inuit fisherman hauls his catch from one of the maze of channels in the delta.

The Arctic has many faces. Compare this flat and monotonous shoreline at the Tuktoyaktuk sandspit in the Western Arctic with the mountainous cliffs of Baffin and Bylot islands to the east.

ABOVE: *The soggy shoreline near Tuktoyaktuk is an eerie land composed of bog, sand, and silt.*

RIGHT: *The bald tundra gives way to a sparse coverlet of scrub forest as the delta slowly merges with the Arctic coastline.*

ABOVE: *Tuktoyaktuk's graveyard lies on the rim of the delta.*

LEFT: *The Inuit know the channels of the delta as well as southern Canadians know the side streets of their hometowns. But a stranger could lose himself in this serpentine maze.*

These odd, cone-shaped mounds, known as
pingos, each more than one hundred feet high,
are peculiar to the delta shoreline. They erupt out
of the silt, looking like miniature volcanoes and
covered with lake-bottom vegetation, but their
core is solid blue ice. They appear to have sprouted
from the old lake bottom rather like frozen milk
emerging from a bottle. That's as good an
explanation as scientists have been able to offer.

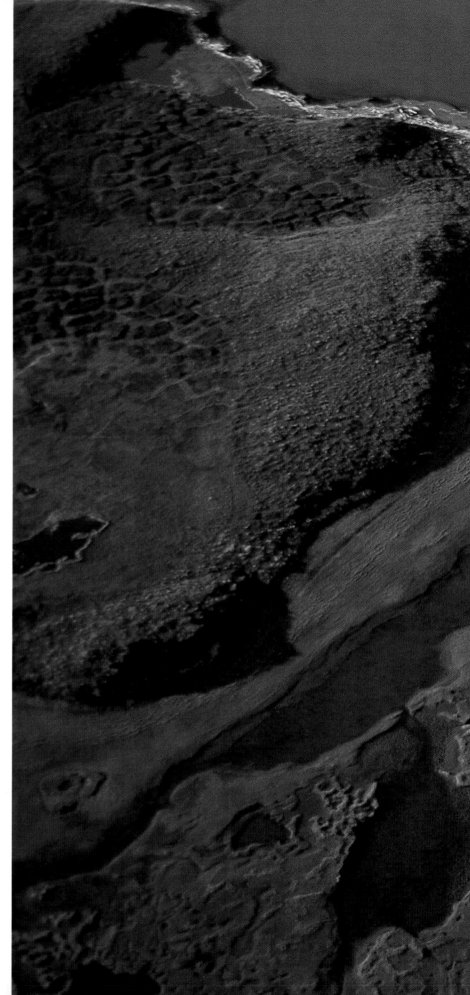

SEA SHAPES

André Gallant uses his camera as a painter uses a brush to delineate
abstract forms along the margins of three oceans.

Cabot Trail, Cape Breton, Nova Scotia.

THE ATLANTIC COAST

WE TEND TO THINK OF THE ATLANTIC COAST AS HARSH AND UNFORGIVING; in many ways it is. Jacques Cartier saw it as "a land of stones, frightful and ill-shaped" when he first touched land off Blanc-Sablon in the Strait of Belle Isle in 1534. The Labrador coast, certainly, accepts its reputation. "If you survive here you are entitled to live by your own standards," David Sinclair, a Labrador journalist, confided to the *National Geographic* in 1993.

Those of us brought up on Kipling's *Captains Courageous* cannot easily erase the image of rugged men in sou'westers battling the elements. But there is more to the Atlantic shore than that. For, like most seagirt realms, this is a land of contrasts. Cartier commented that he hadn't seen a carload of soil on the first shores he visited, but when he moved on to the northwest coast of Prince Edward Island, with its rich forests of cedars, yews, and pines, he revised his earlier impressions.

The soil is a problem. Much of New Brunswick's is coarse and stony. Newfoundland's thin layer is short of nutrients. Nova Scotia and Prince Edward Island tend to be one-crop regions—apples from the former, potatoes from the latter. There is good land here for tree growing, as the early ship-builders found, but not much else.

Yet the coast also harbours some of the most picturesque settings in Canada, as the photographs following page 212 demonstrate.

The real wealth lies a few fathoms beneath the sea in the shallow banks that stretch out from the coast for more than 125 miles. Here, submerged beneath the myriad islands, lies another "island"—the famous Grand Banks, forming part of a continental shelf that is five times as broad as its Pacific counterpart.

Into this vast and fertile undersea world man himself has ventured hoping to uncover a treasure as great as the ten thousand tons of bottom feeders that are lifted daily from the Grand Banks. Oil has been discovered here, and the people of the Atlantic hold their breath. It is just possible that these new discoveries may serve to redress the balance upset by the wanton destruction of the Atlantic's other great natural resource, the northern cod.

CHAPTER SEVEN

THE GOLDEN AGE OF SAIL

IN THE MID-NINETEENTH CENTURY, WHEN THE GOLDEN AGE BEGAN, THE FORESTS of the East Coast stretched to the very margin of the sea, creating two great exports for New Brunswick, Nova Scotia, Prince Edward Island, and Newfoundland. The first major export was timber; the second was the wooden vessel that carried the first across the ocean. In scores of sequestered coves, new vessels were literally hacked out of the softwood forests, loaded with pine and spruce from the adjacent timber-land, and then sent to Europe to be sold off with their cargoes. Wooden sailing vessels were the first great manufactured export of the Atlantic communities.

Thus was the timber trade tied symbiotically to the craft of shipbuilding. The earliest shipowners were also timber merchants. The carriers—schooners, barques, barquentines, brigs, brigantines, and, later, big three-masted square-riggers—were cheaply built of softwood, without blueprints, by a handful of experienced artisans handy with axe and auger. The only machinery required was a sawmill built on the spot and a blacksmithing outfit.

The inexpensive vessels did not endure, but they laid the groundwork for some of the great Canadian fortunes, such as that of Izaak Walton Killam, said to have been the richest Canadian of his day, whose death duties were so enormous that the prime minister used them to subsidize the Canada Council in 1957. Thus, hundreds of writers, painters, and other artists owe their careers to the boom days of wooden ships and iron men.

The boom began in 1850, with the Australian gold rush following hard in the wake of the California stampede. The world went gold crazy. As Frederick William Wallace, the Maritime historian, has written, "Ships, ships, and more ships! was the cry." With the British yards unable to keep up with the demand, the Liverpool shipowners began to look over the big timber-droghers coming in from British North America, their owners eager to sell both ships and cargoes.

As the golden age rolled on, the Maritime yards began to turn out larger and larger vessels for transoceanic service. The most famous was the *Marco Polo*, a 184-foot-long three-decker, stoutly constructed of hackmatack (larch), pine, and oak ripped from the forest surrounding Saint John. She was the biggest and fastest vessel of her day, a roomy, heavily timbered ship, designed to pack a large cargo. She was no clipper, but she made the run to Liverpool in a surprising fifteen days and was later sold for a fat profit to the Black Ball Line. Her new owners fitted her out as a luxury packet on the Australia run.

The Bluenose, *world's fastest and most famous fishing schooner, at the peak of her career.*

Thus metamorphosed, she set off for the South Seas on July 4, 1852, under the command of the famous captain James Nichol "Bully" Forbes, who arrogantly boasted that he'd have her back on the Mersey within six months. Forbes's rivals scoffed at that, but *Marco Polo* beat the steamer *Australia* by a week on the trip out. In order to prevent his crew from deserting for the goldfields, Forbes had them clapped into prison on a trumped-up charge until *Marco Polo* was ready to sail for home.

Forbes was a bold and skilful mariner of unbounded nerve, notorious for squeezing the fastest time out of ships not built for speed. Once, when he was driving one of his vessels through a strong gale, a deputation of passengers pleaded with him to shorten sail. "Hell or Melbourne!" the doughty captain cried, a phrase that went into the nautical lexicon.

A half-finished ship rests on the stocks at West Advocate, N.S., in the great era of shipbuilding.

A diminutive redhead with scarred, ruddy features, Forbes had been at sea since the age of twelve. With his crew out of jail, he left Melbourne on October 11, 1852, and was back on the Mersey after a record passage of seventy-six days. The round trip had taken an unprecedented five months and twenty-one days, astounding the shipping world and making Forbes a national hero. Thousands poured down to the docks to cheer the huge banner between the *Marco Polo*'s masts announcing that she was THE FASTEST SHIP IN THE WORLD. As she set off on a second voyage, Forbes issued a second boast to his passengers: "Ladies and gentlemen, last trip I astonished the world with the sailing of this ship. This time I intend to astonish God Almighty."

Under Forbes and his successors, *Marco Polo* continued to astonish. Other shipyards tried to duplicate her, but none matched her record. As late as 1867 she was still able to make the Melbourne–Liverpool run in seventy-six days. She ended her life as a tramp, and in 1883, caught in a gale, she piled up on Cape Cavendish, Prince Edward Island, and was lost. Forbes, who had an equally distinguished career, had already died at the age of fifty-two. On his tombstone was carved a short epitaph: *Master of the famous* Marco Polo.

The golden age continued for thirty years. The size and number of vessels built on the Atlantic coast increased decade by decade. On average, ships of the 1880s were four times larger than those of the twenties. The Maritime fleet soared to a total of 7,500 vessels, the Newfoundland fleet to an additional 1,600. By 1878 Canada had the fourth-largest merchant marine in the world, just behind the fleets of Great Britain, the United States, and Norway. The Atlantic coast was the centre of the industry, accounting for 72 percent of all tonnage registered.

By this time, sailing vessels were not only part of the Maritime economy but also part of the culture. The Atlantic colonies lived by producing and exporting such staple products as timber, fish, and sealskins, but the chief manufactured export was shipping. Fuelled by immigration, the boom roared on. By the early 1870s some fifteen thousand people worked directly in the fleets of Atlantic Canada while the shipping industry almost equalled the lumber business in economic terms.

In the 1870s Nova Scotia forged ahead to become the leading shipbuilding and shipowning province on the Atlantic coast. The fleet numbered 825 square-riggers, turning such ports as Halifax and Yarmouth into forests of masts and canvas. The various harbours were crammed with windjammers—as many as eighty loading timber in Saint John alone. The largest wooden square-rigged ship ever built in British North America was launched at Maitland, Nova Scotia, in 1874. Her owner, William Davidson Lawrence, for whom she was named, laid the keel—244 feet, 9 inches long, making her the largest sailing ship in the world.

Nothing that size had been attempted since 1855, when the Wrights of Saint John launched the *Morning Light*, then the finest and most expensive ship of her day. The *Lawrence* was twenty feet longer and her tonnage slightly greater. She was no clipper but "a great ark of a vessel designed to pack cargo."

Her owner was eager to see what she could do when given a chance and on her first voyage urged her captain to push her to the limit. She was already making fifteen knots and the captain wanted to reduce canvas, but Lawrence, who was also the skipper's father-in-law, would have none of it. "Hold on a bit until the log reads sixteen knots," he advised. "She'll make it." Shortly afterward, the ship dived into a big sea, losing her three topmasts and yards in a thundering crash. Sweating in the swells for hour after hour, her crew toiled to clear the fouled mass of stays and running gear, sails, and rigging tackles and to heave the spars back on board. The following day, working in the stormiest seas in the world, they managed at last to send the topmasts and top gallants aloft.

In 1883, Lawrence's hard-driving son took the helm, and made such a rapid passage that the ship cleared an extra thousand dollars profit. His father made him a present of the money. On that trip, Wallace, the Maritime historian, tells us, "Captain Lawrence drove her like a madman, cracking on and carrying sail until he had his crew scared stiff." He sprang a foremast, but her performance was so good that his father was able to sell the ship to a Norwegian buyer for $86,000.

By then the great days of the square-rigger were already in decline. By the turn of the century, shipbuilding and shipping in the Atlantic ports had collapsed. It was easy enough to blame the emergence of steam and the switch to iron vessels,

In scores of sequestered coves, new vessels were literally hacked out of the softwood forests, loaded with pine and spruce from the adjacent timberland, and then sent to Europe to be sold off with their cargoes.

167

but other nations had no difficulty in switching to steam and iron. Why not the Canadian Maritimers?

In the words of two leading Maritime historians, Eric W. Sager and Gerald E. Panting, "the golden age of sail . . . was doomed not by the inevitable advance of technology or by impersonal market factors but by the Maritimers themselves." In their study of Maritime capital, they note "the pervasive pessimism that became a self-fulfilling prophecy." The Maritimers could not or would not adapt. The ship-builders were merchant traders first and shipowners second. When profits declined they sought opportunities elsewhere. As Sager has written (in a second work, with Lewis B. Fischer), "To an increasing number of old merchants and their sons, it seemed that the future lay with railways, textiles, sugar refineries, iron and steel . . . ."

By the 1880s the eyes of the nation had turned westward. The government was more interested in subsidizing the new railways than in providing bounties for ship-building. A large chunk of Maritime capital was tied up in wooden ships while Ontario was investing heavily in railways, iron foundries, and machine shops. As early as 1870 the industrial output per capita in that province was 60 percent greater than in the two leading Maritime provinces.

Earlier in the century one Maritimer had understood the possibilities of steam power and iron ships. Samuel Cunard was a diminutive merchant whose slightness of figure belied compelling energy. His father, Abraham, a descendant of German Quaker immigrants, had entered the timber and West Indian trade out of Halifax in 1812. At that time, no one, certainly not Samuel or Abraham Cunard, dreamed that steam vessels would ever threaten the big windjammers. But by 1831, Samuel, now head of the family firm, had changed his mind. The arrival in Halifax of the 160-foot steamer *Royal William*, "a great Leviathan of the sea," convinced him that "steamers properly built and manned might start and arrive at their destination with the punctuality of railway trains on land."

The concept of an "ocean railway" across the Atlantic fitted the changing times, for the rail lines introduced a new idea into North America—that of punctuality. The big square-riggers were slaves to the vagrant winds, but the early side-wheelers could leave port and arrive to a tight schedule. For the first time, His Majesty's mails would be on time.

Cunard obtained a contract to run a weekly mail service between Pictou, Nova Scotia, and Charlottetown and ordered two steamers for that purpose. Significantly,

Three-masters, built from lumber often hewn on the spot, became timber carriers themselves and were regularly sold in English ports, cargo and all, providing the Atlantic provinces with their two greatest exports. These are Ladysmith, Eva C., *and* Harry W. Lewis.

they were built in Scotland. The Maritimers did not have the know-how; their experience was confined to wood and sail. By January 1841, Cunard had four new steamers in regular year-round service between Liverpool, Halifax, and Boston.

That was the start of the great Cunard Line, whose steamers, by the time of Samuel's death in 1865, were known as the Queens of the Ocean. Ironically, Cunard died almost at the height of sail's golden age, but by 1907, when the steam-powered *Mauretania* and *Lusitania*—the biggest, fastest, and most powerful ships on the Atlantic—were launched, the days of the square-riggers were no more than a memory.

The only survivor was the cargo schooner, which prevailed well into the twentieth century. Adapted for use in dangerous northern waters and along the lengthy coastlines, this was usually a two-masted vessel built for fishing, for the seal hunt, for coastal trading, and for longer voyages to the West Indies and South America. By 1857 the three-masted "tern" schooner had made its appearance, its numbers increasing annually after 1880. In the peak year of 1919 no fewer than 114 three- and four-masters were built—sleek craft, cheaply designed—to export local products: lumber, fish, gypsum. No steamer could compete with them. They required smaller crews than the larger vessels and, thanks to their fore-and-aft rigging, could

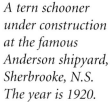

A tern schooner under construction at the famous Anderson shipyard, Sherbrooke, N.S. The year is 1920.

manoeuvre more easily along the ragged coastline. They were cheaper to build and operate than the larger ships, and their cargoes were usually loaded in a single port. Losses from World War I sparked a brief postwar building boom, but after 1919, cargo schooner construction dwindled to a finish.

Fishing schooners, however, continued to be turned out at such ports as Lunenburg until the 1940s and 1950s, when they were replaced by motorized trawlers. Though built of softwood, mainly spruce, many had long working lives, as was the case with the *W. A. Knock*, built in 1923 and in service until she was destroyed by fire at sea thirty-five years later. Very few survived to rot away on the Maritime beaches. Most were shipwrecked, abandoned, or sold to others who eventually lost them to the ravages of rocks, wind, and waves.

Many have long since been forgotten, but two have made the history books. One was the notorious rumrunner *I'm Alone*, the other the spectacularly famous racing schooner *Bluenose*.

During the prohibition days, rumrunning was considered a legitimate business, one that helped boost the schooner trade in the years after the Great War. St. Pierre and Miquelon, the French possessions off Newfoundland's south coast, became an important base for the business. There, Canadian schooners loaded up legally with liquor and carried it to the offshore limits of U.S. territorial waters, where fast launches picked it up and ferried it to shore. As long as the Canadian schooners stayed beyond the limit, they were safe from the U.S. Coast Guard. If they ventured over the line they could be seized and even sunk.

In March 1929, *I'm Alone*, equipped with powerful auxiliary engines and loaded with whisky, made international headlines when she was overtaken and sunk by two American coast guard cutters. She was registered in Lunenburg but owned by a dummy company controlled by American bootleggers whose principal was a big, genial two-hundred-pounder known as Big Jamie Clarke. Big Jamie hired an equally colourful skipper, a much-decorated Newfoundlander named John Thomas Randall. A resident of Lunenburg, Jack Randall was something of a fashion plate. His kit aboard *I'm Alone* included a dinner jacket, tailcoat, six dress shirts, a dozen dress collars, and eighteen pairs of silk socks.

When the American cutter signalled the schooner to heave to, the captain seized a battered bullhorn and shouted, "I'll see you in Hell first!" He had been shuttling cargoes of whisky between the port of Belize and the Louisiana coast and thought himself safely beyond the international limit. The Americans thought differently and after a long parley opened fire. Shells and bullets pierced the vessel's rigging; others smashed windows, hull, and engines. The schooner took on water so

The days of the square-riggers were no more than a memory. The only survivor was the cargo schooner, which prevailed well into the twentieth century

swiftly that by the time Randall ordered his crew to abandon ship, her foredeck was level with the sea. One man drowned, the others were rescued, and Canada was faced with a full-fledged international incident.

The controversy raged in the press until an international commission was appointed to rule on the case. The decision didn't come until January 5, 1935, when the commissioners concluded that although the schooner's business was unlawful, the coast guard's action was unlawful, too. The United States, issuing a formal apology, paid out $25,000 as a token of regret and a similar sum in compensation to the crew. Randall got an additional seven thousand for the loss of his job and his gear, which had included, as part of his extensive wardrobe, a collapsible opera hat.

But even as the *I'm Alone* case was giving Canada a black eye in the United States, another Lunenburg vessel, *Bluenose*, was making headlines of a different kind. She was a working fishing schooner, built for speed and designed by Bill Roué, a soda-pop bottler from Halifax whose ambition was to be a naval architect. "Sure," he said affably, when a committee of local businessmen approached him, "I'll try my hand at a schooner."

And what a schooner! When she was launched on March 26, 1921, before a huge crowd, the mood was electric. She was exactly what the sponsors had hoped: a beautiful black vessel, 130.2 feet long, twenty-seven feet wide—a leading candidate to win the International Fisherman's Trophy for Canada. Her skipper would be another Lunenburg fisherman, the fiery, demanding Angus Walters. As Silver Donald Cameron has written, "So began a remarkable marriage of man and ship, which ultimately made Angus Walters the most famous fisherman on earth."

That October she beat the American champion, *Elsie*, in two straight races. The following year she humbled the *Henry Ford*, two out of three. In 1923 she beat the "most beautiful of all the Gloucester racers," *Columbia*, only to be disqualified on a technicality. The series was suspended for eight years.

She went fishing, made money for her owners, and survived uncounted gales and a near fatal hurricane off Sable Island. An old boat by 1930, ineptly repaired after running aground off Newfoundland, she raced the crack *Gertrude L. Thebaud* of Gloucester and lost. Back in shape the following year, she raced the *Thebaud* for the international championship and won handily.

She was due for retirement. In 1938, Walters took on the *Thebaud* in a final contest, hoping a win would ensure that his schooner would be preserved as a national treasure. It was, as Cameron has written, a no-holds-barred contest, with each schooner winning two of the first four races. In the final race, "the *Bluenose* sailed as though the Gods themselves were within her . . . Sprinting over the finish line at Boston, she evoked an awestruck silence and then a great roar of admiration as her rival conceded that 'she was, and deserved to be, the champion—forever.'"

In a later era she might have been preserved as a monument to the great days of the schooners. Instead she was sold, ending her years in a collision with a Haitian reef. It wasn't until 1960 that Walters persuaded the Oland Breweries to build a replica to advertise their Schooner brand of beer. The *Bluenose II* was launched to a tumultuous celebration in the summer of 1963. The province later bought her for a dollar and mounted a national campaign to raise a quarter-million to refit her. Now in private hands and again refitted, immortalized by her image on the back of the Canadian ten-cent piece, she stands as a living symbol of all the tall ships that roamed the Atlantic coastline and crossed the furious oceans during the golden age of sail.

The four-masted schooner Cutty Sark *under construction at Saint John, N.B., near the end of the nineteenth century.*

HISTORIC LUNENBURG

The British peopled Lunenburg in 1753, with some 1,400 German-speaking "foreign Protestants" to balance Nova Scotia's largely Acadian population. Thanks to its distinctive nineteenth-century architecture, the Old Town has been declared a National Historic District and also a World Heritage Site—right up there with the pyramids and the Taj Mahal.

ABOVE: An old-style wrought-iron anchor forms a door knocker on the nearest of the Pelham Street houses.

RIGHT: These typical houses with projecting bay windows, facing on Pelham Street, go back before the turn of the century.

174

ABOVE: *The upper floors of the Bluenose Lodge, one of the most prominent buildings in New Town. Note the Gothic dormer.*

LEFT: *Boscawen Manor, built in the Queen Anne style* circa 1888, *its asymmetrical form emphasized by a circular tower. Now being revitalized after several years of decline, it is one of the town's few surviving "mansions."*

ABOVE: *Rear view of 367 Pelham Street, said to have been built in 1828 by George Anderson, a blacksmith. The house has been kept remarkably intact in its nineteenth-century form.*

LEFT: *The entranceway of a 1900 building at 224 Pelham Street. The tall central doorway, trimmed with massive pilasters and deep transom window, is the focus of the main façade.*

ABOVE: *Close view of a simple waterfront building painted in the traditional red. The paint, made from red ochre and linseed oil, was chosen because it was available and cheap.*

RIGHT: *A view of the Lunenburg waterfront with the red Fisheries Museum of the Atlantic in the left foreground. This was formerly the Lunenburg Sea Products building. Note the three church towers in the distance surrounded by clusters of variously shaped and colourful buildings.*

LEFT: *This large double house was built in 1915, "a good example of the straightforward unpretentious housing of the era," in the words of William Plaskett, who compiled the inventory of the town's historic buildings. The diamond-shaped window separates the two main doors of the house.*

ABOVE AND RIGHT: *Details of the Zwicker House. Originally a Georgian style building, circa 1830, it was later Victorianized. The detailing is impressive, and with its round-topped windows and ornate tower, the exterior composition today is more Italianate than Georgian.*

CHAPTER EIGHT

WHAT HAPPENED TO THE COD?

SINCE THE AUGUST DAY IN 1497 WHEN THE EXPLORER JOHN CABOT RETURNED TO Bristol harbour from the New World to report that the Atlantic coast was swarming with fish, cod has been the cornerstone—nay, the lifeblood—of Newfoundland's economy. Until the 1980s, the waters off the Grand Banks teemed with cod—so many that the supply was deemed inexhaustible. Some thirty-five thousand people derived their living, directly or indirectly, from East Coast cod, which represented 10 percent of the world's entire catch and helped make Canada the world's largest exporter of fish.

In one way or another, cod has impinged on the lives of all of us, from the cod-liver oil we swallowed as children during the sunless days of a Canadian winter to the fish and chips we still enjoy during the palmy days of summer. The graphic symbol of a man in a sou'wester hauling a gigantic codfish on his back is part of the country's iconography. I remember it from childhood imprinted on the labels of the Scott's Emulsion bottles as I swallowed my daily tablespoonful. Newfoundland without cod? One might as well posit a Canada without maple syrup!

But on July 2, 1992, with the celebratory clamour of Canada's 125th birthday party still ringing in his ears, John Crosbie, then minister of fisheries and oceans, conceded a fact that he had earlier tried to deny but that a small group of scientists and inshore fisherman had already realized: the cod were gone. The situation was so desperate that all commercial fishing was outlawed for two years, a moratorium that had to be extended and is still in force. The shock that followed was like an earthquake: hard to believe, difficult to explain, not easy to accept. Since that time some Maritimers have talked wistfully of the "return" of the cod, as if some pelagic pied piper has spirited them away temporarily to lurk in an obscure backwater before returning to the fish pastures of Newfoundland. It is exactly that kind of wishful thinking that lies behind the original decline of the East Coast's greatest natural resource.

OPPOSITE: The days when a giant cod could dwarf a small boy are long gone. One of these was five feet long and weighed sixty pounds. Both were caught in a trap at Battle Harbour, Labrador.

Like the salmon fishers of the West Coast and the prodigal whale hunters of the Arctic, human predators plundered the Atlantic of its bounty with little thought for the future, believing, against all evidence, that the supply of cod was limitless. And so it seemed to be for the best part of five centuries. When Cabot returned to England, the Duke of Milan's London envoy reported that the explorer had found cod so plentiful that they "can be taken not only with the net but in baskets let down with a stone so that it sinks in the water." Whether or not Cabot actually said this,

we do know that the Atlantic coast was alive with codfish of size and quantity never before witnessed by Europeans. The cod rush was on. By the end of the sixteenth century, Plymouth harbour alone was white with the fluttering canvas of fifty two-masted Newfoundland fishing craft. The scramble for cod did not abate for another four centuries, and small wonder—cod is to the Atlantic what cedar and salmon have been to the Pacific, a resource that helped shape the social pattern of a province.

We have all eaten cod, if only in the form of supermarket fish sticks. It is a delicious, nutritious fish; at least 95 percent of it is edible. Even the skin has been used to make a kind of leather for pouches. There is scarcely any fat on its bones—less than three-tenths of one percent. Eighteen percent of a freshly caught cod is protein, 80 percent when the water is squeezed out and the fish is dried. It can be cured, dried, salted, smoked, canned, and, since the 1950s, fast frozen. Thus it is easy

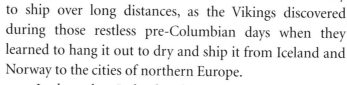

to ship over long distances, as the Vikings discovered during those restless pre-Columbian days when they learned to hang it out to dry and ship it from Iceland and Norway to the cities of northern Europe.

In those days Iceland and Greenland were within the northern range of the Atlantic cod. It sustained the Vikings on their peripatetic travels to "Stoneland," "Woodland," and "Vineland," one of which was probably Newfoundland, since evidence of their passing has been found on the island's northern tip.

Cod is not a sportsman's fish. It does not struggle, let alone give battle, as a salmon does. It is easy to catch, as my

A boatload of codfish caught in the Gulf of St. Lawrence in the days before the larger ones were depleted.

smaller children discovered in 1967 in the shallow coastal waters off Prince Edward Island. All you do is drop a weighted line over the side and haul the fish up from the bottom. The cod will eat anything that moves, swallowing any fish or man-made lure that will fit into its mouth. It lurks in the shallows, not far from the shore, its skin mottled like the sand and gravel dropped on the coastal shelves by the retreating glaciers. After the ice vanished and human fishers arrived, the cod swam innocently into unbaited traps of twine netting anchored to the rocky coast each summer.

Though it is easy enough to catch, the cod is a survivor and has been for at least ten million years. When the great ice sheets covered Canada's East Coast, the cod simply escaped south to return when the ice retreated. The geology of the Atlantic coast provides a perfect environment for this durable fish. In glacial times the ocean levels were much lower than they are today because so much water was frozen. The continental shelf rose out of the sea, a flat coastal plain descending gently to the margins of the shrunken ocean. As new rivers and deltas began to crease this plain, a series of low hills and basins was created. When the ice sheet melted and the waters rose again, these contours were submerged to form those sections of the continental shelf known as "banks." Here, off the coasts of Newfoundland and Nova Scotia, the chill Labrador Current sweeps down from the north to collide with the warmer Gulf Stream, providing a perfect environment for the plankton, small shrimp, and capelin on which cod at various stages of development feed.

The greatest of all the underwater pastures are the Grand Banks off the southeast coast of Newfoundland, larger than the province itself. Here, in the sunlit, shallow waters, no more than a few hundred feet deep, these mottled bottom feeders live and breed in the ancient gravels. They are prodigious spawners. In the old abundant days, schools of spawning cod contained hundreds of millions of fish. Even as late as 1992 the width of one such school seen north of the Grand Banks was estimated at a mile and a half. A spawning female can produce at least two million eggs, and, in the case of larger fish, as many as eleven million. But only one egg in a million reaches maturity, which is perhaps just as well. Otherwise the cod might easily choke the oceans.

Today, the East Coast faces a diametrically different question: too few cod, not too many, a dilemma that the federal government has blindly refused to face. As late as 1989, John Crosbie, himself a Newfoundlander, managed to put the blame on outside influences: the increasing seal population brought on by the animal rights movement; overfishing by foreigners outside the two-hundred-mile limit; and changes in ocean temperature. Though all these factors contributed to the controversy, they were really minor issues, peripheral to the real problem: omnipresent human greed.

The sad, indeed scandalous, story of the vanishing cod is a tale of political obfuscation, wrong assumptions, unreliable data, overly optimistic predictions, bad science, and massive overfishing in Canadian waters caused by technological advances and a federal authority that lacked the will and courage to conserve fish stocks. It was politically more popular to save jobs than to save the fish that produced those jobs.

Conservation was not a problem in the nineteenth century. The three-hundred-year-old techniques used by Grand Banks fishermen could scarcely dent the cod population. Cod fishing was rather like sport fishing. You stood in your boat, or in a barrel lashed to the deck, and you dropped a dozen hooked lines over the side. With a five-hundred-foot hemp line you could catch a hundred or so cod in a day and as many as four hundred on a very good day. The fishers stayed close to the shore, returning home the same day to cure their fish, which were split open and

Cod has impinged on the lives of all of us, from the cod-liver oil we swallowed as children during the sunless days of a Canadian winter to the fish and chips we still enjoy during the palmy days of summer.

spread out on the rocky beach. To be sure, the development of the two-man dory, a twenty-foot deckless vessel, and the two-masted schooner, both of which came to symbolize the Newfoundland fishery, increased the size of the catch. And early in the nineteenth century, the French longline, or "trawl line," with a baited hook at three-foot intervals, made it possible to catch cod in quantity at a distance of four or five miles from shore. In spite of such advances, however, the cod still flourished.

British biologist Thomas Henry Huxley, who sat on three fishing commissions, scoffed at suggestions to restrict longlining by law. In a remarkable statement to the International Fisheries Exhibition of 1883 that was quoted over the years as gospel, Huxley declared that "any tendency to over-fishing will meet its natural check in the diminution of supply. . . This check will always come into operation long before anything like permanent exhaustion has occurred." The cod fishery, Huxley declared, "and probably all great sea fisheries are inexhaustible; that is to say that nothing we can do seriously affects the number of fish." Those reassuring words were echoed two years later in a Canadian ministry of agriculture report. Referring to Huxley, it declared that it would be impossible to exhaust the commercial fishing resources or "even noticeably to lessen their number by the means now used for their capture."

Those means would change with the technological achievements of the next century. When steam replaced sail, and later when diesel power replaced steam, the trawl lines could be dragged farther and farther from the coastline. But this was a development fostered by outsiders. The Grand Banks fleet stuck with sail. The schooner, the net trap, the dory, and the longline remained the basis of Canadian technology well into the twentieth century. Using these techniques, individual entrepreneurs were able to land 330,000 tons of cod annually without damaging the environment or reducing the fish population.

The big change came from Europe in the 1950s with the arrival of the stern draggers: huge vessels, each as long as a football field, that hauled in their wakes great bag-like nets held open by steel plates, heavy chains, and rollers that played havoc with the ocean floor. Equipped with electronic devices to locate the fish, they churned their way through the dense spawning grounds at a time when the cod were highly vulnerable to capture, dispersing the milt and eggs and reducing even further the chances of fertilization. Because they operated beyond the twelve-mile limit, the draggers were independent of Canadian law.

Cod by the hundred dry out on a Halifax wharf, helping provide the Maritimes with one of its biggest exports. This photograph suggests why fishermen thought the supply was unlimited.

The new fast-freezing techniques were combined with the dragger technology to produce the huge factory ships that came from countries thousands of miles away—from Germany, Great Britain, Spain, Portugal, Poland, the Soviet Union, Cuba, and even as far east as Asia—to plunder the ocean just twelve miles from Canadian shores.

The first of these was the British *Fairtry*, launched in 1954. A 2,640-ton vessel, more than 275 feet long, she was several times larger than the biggest trawler of her day, but she would soon be dwarfed by much larger factory ships. She was so successful that her huge net sometimes gave way under the weight of the fish that were winched up to her stern. "Nothing is more provoking," her captain reported, "than to see this happen or the cod end burst and the sea covered with dying flesh."

In these monstrous vessels—the largest displaced 8,128 tons—the freshly caught cod were immediately filleted and frozen. That meant the factory ship could stay out for a fortnight and catch tons of fish. The figures are daunting. In the sixteenth century a fisher could count himself fortunate to land a hundred tons in a season. But a factory ship could land that much in an hour. Before 1954, the annual catch off Labrador and the Grand Banks amounted to some 355,600 tons. In the record year of 1968 that figure had reached 823,000. As one writer has pointed out,

Salt cod being weighed for export in the good old days when this was a staple product.

"In the space of two decades we let foreign ships all but wipe out one of our great natural resources."

The enormous fish—the kind depicted on the Scott's Emulsion label—were gone. In his definitive biography of "Cod," Mark Kurlansky wrote of going out from Petty Harbour with two fishing boats from Continental Fishery (now the only legal cod fishery in Newfoundland) kept in operation for scientific purposes. One boat was for tagging fish. The other boat was to catch one hundred fish for examination by sex and age. But the taggers could find only forty fish, and only three of these were large enough to be capable of spawning. The average weight of those caught by the other boat was less than four pounds. In the old days it would have been at least ten.

For years the inshore fishers complained about the intense pressure of the factory ships. Nobody listened. By 1975 the annual catch had dwindled from the record 823,000 to less than 305,000 tons. At last the government woke up and in 1976 extended its jurisdiction to two hundred miles. That effectively ended foreign cod fishing in its waters.

Now, with the factory ships gone and the annual catch reduced to 141,200 tons, Canada had a God-given chance to save the cod by capping the catch at that figure and allowing the species to regenerate. Astonishingly, it did nothing of the sort. Instead, against the advice of a majority of fishers, the Canadian government decided to have its own dragger fleet. At a cost of millions of dollars, it bailed out National Sea Products of Halifax and Fishery Products International of St. John's and provided these two companies with almost half the total available fish quotas. By 1979 the resulting massive corporate dragger fleet was ready for the spawning grounds. Corporate profit, not conservation, was the priority.

The draggers wanted only the largest and most valuable fish. When the mass of struggling cod was winched to the surface in the big nets, the small, unprofitable fish were tossed overboard and left to die. A 1986 government report estimated that sixteen million cod were destroyed by the two companies in one eight-week period. Here, if ever, was a case of long-term pain for short-term gain. By the winter of 1991 the two firms discovered there weren't enough fish left in the spawning grounds to make a profit. In attempting to support a new Maritime industry, the government had presided over the destruction of a natural resource—one that had survived for 450 years without quotas, rules, or regulations.

From the 1970s, the Department of Fisheries and Oceans consistently overestimated the stock of available cod and set the TAC (Total Allowable Catch) quota far higher than scientific advice suggested. In 1977, the department forecast that the TAC would soar to a healthy 408,000 tons by 1985. That starry-eyed projection led

For years the inshore fishermen complained about the intense pressure of the factory ships. By 1975 the annual catch had dwindled from the record 823,000 to less than 305,000 tons.

to the rapid expansion of an overly optimistic fishing industry. But by 1985 the department was forced to backpedal. It had to reduce its 1985 forecast to 270,000 tons—a disastrous discrepancy of 34 percent.

And yet the fisheries department continued to predict larger quantities of cod than actually existed and to set quotas far too high. Although the DFO kept insisting that the stock was growing, its own biologists, using what is known as the Virtual Population Analysis, knew better. If anything, the cod population was declining. Nonetheless the department found that jobs were politically more important than fish.

It should have been obvious from the figures available that too many cod were being caught and that year after year the fishing quotas were being set too high. In 1989 it was clear to scientists that the total year's catch should be limited to 127,000 tons if the cod population were to remain stable. Instead, the minister boosted the level to 238,700 tons—a devastating figure—"in order not to disrupt the industry." But the industry was disrupted anyway by the 1992 moratorium, which made it clear that all the optimistic projections had been nothing more than a sham.

It was not until the summer of 1997 that the real story came to light. For years before the moratorium, the government had been in the business of distorting and suppressing the truth about the destruction of Newfoundland cod. That was the embarrassing conclusion of an internal report commissioned by Newfoundland's regional science director and distributed internally in 1993. It did not come to public attention until 1997, when a copy fell into the hands of the Canadian Press.

In the years before the cod stocks collapsed, the report stated, the federal government had twisted the findings of fisheries scientists to suit its political agenda. "Scientific information surrounding the cod moratorium, specifically the role of the environment, was gruesomely mangled and corrupted to meet political ends," the report stated, adding that "many scientists wondered what had happened to their conclusions."

The report said that fisheries department scientists were routinely gagged while "ill-informed" spokespersons conveyed false information to the public, emphasizing the role of seals and changing water temperature—not overfishing— in the cod's disappearance. "Management is fostering an attitude of scientific deception, misinformation and obfuscation, in presenting and defending the science that the department undertakes and the results it achieves."

Ottawa even went so far as to dispatch "scouting missions at the expense of planned valid scientific research" in order to help the industry and to back the official line that fish stocks were healthy. "It has become far too convenient for resource managers and others to publicly state that their decisions were based on scientific advice when this was not the case," the report stated.

Blaming the government hasn't brought back the northern cod, though it may stop some of the politicians from grasping at straws. Brian Tobin, Newfoundland's new premier, was no sooner in office than he made the harp seal the scapegoat again for the cod's decline. Indeed, any casual newspaper reader might have been led to believe that the crisis was over. On its front page in October 1996, the *Globe and Mail* carried a story headlined "Cod coming back, fishermen say," certainly giving that impression. That report referred only to the south coast of the province, yet it was enough to make the new fisheries minister, Fred Mifflin, jubilant. "The fish are fatter, they are healthier, so we know for sure the decline has ceased," he declared. Within a fortnight he was being asked to take a calculated risk and allow some fishing on the south coast—in effect, to chip away at the moratorium. In April 1997 he did just that. In spite of protests by scientists he bowed to pressure and announced that two cod fisheries, one on the Gulf of St. Lawrence, the other in southern Newfoundland, would be re-opened with annual allowable catches of 6,096 and 10,160 tons respectively. The move was politically popular but, as anyone who has studied the history of the cod's decline must realize, such short-term policies can only lead to longer-term disaster.

Fishermen in harbour at Souris, Prince Edward Island. The year was 1910, when few gave a thought to conservation.

WORK AND PLAY AT THE CENTURY'S TURN

When lobsters were cheap and bathing costumes were voluminous.

ABOVE: A lobsterman poses with a specimen in 1910.

RIGHT: The people of the Atlantic have always made good use of their coastline—the longest in Canada. Here, in this century-old photograph, a family squishes through the tidal flats searching for mollusks.

ABOVE: *A touring car at Portugal Cove, Newfoundland.* "*Touring*" *was a popular form of Sunday recreation.*

RIGHT: *A diving party aboard H.M.S.* Blake, *circa 1895, long before the word* "*scuba*" *entered the language.*

Diving Party
H.M.S. Ble[...]

In 1890 on Prince Edward Island, young ladies took to the water in "bathing costumes" that seemed revealing only when contrasted with the voluminous dress of their elders.

ABOVE: *Fishing was more than a vocation for Prince Edward Islanders. It also enhanced a vacation for groups like the one above holidaying at Rustico Beach on the north shore.*

LEFT: *The Notman studio made this photograph of a racing cutter's crew practising off Halifax in 1915.*

ABOVE: *A century ago the warm ocean on the north shore of Prince Edward Island provided a playground for vacationers. Even those who didn't "bathe" (to use the accepted term) splashed through the shallows with their shoes off, like small children.*

LEFT: *In 1908, when the supply of cod seem unlimited, these traditional two-masted schooners—shown here off Cape Charles, Labrador, in the narrow Strait of Belle Isle—had no trouble reporting record catches.*

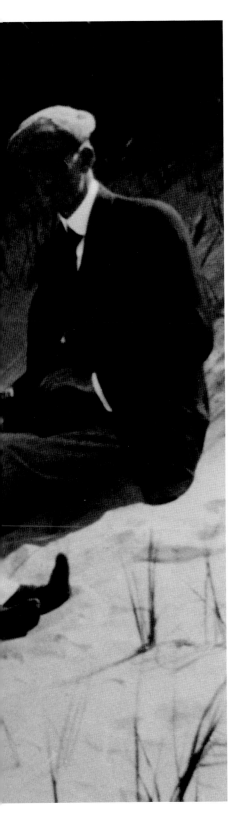

ABOVE: A gigantic tuna, twice the size of the
man who caught it, is photographed for posterity.

LEFT: Members of a family group, dressed
appropriately in what passed for casual clothing
in the first decade of the century, enjoy a picnic
in the sand dunes of Prince Edward Island.

CHAPTER NINE

THE GRAVEYARD OF THE ATLANTIC

L'ILE DE SABLON. . . SABLE ISLAND. . . THE ISLAND OF SAND.

Not an island, really, just a big sandbar, a partially exposed shoal shaped like a fingernail clipping, twenty-five miles long but only a mile wide. It sits alone in the trackless sea, 180 miles southeast of Halifax, a mere pinpoint on the map of the Nova Scotia coast. It looks so innocent, but, for its size, it is the deadliest piece of real estate in the country.

It is solid sand, as if a small chunk of the Sahara had been dropped into the cold Atlantic: no rocks here, no garden soil, no crags, no polished pebbles, no trees, no leafy glades, and no foliage save a thin fringe of low bushes—cranberries and blueberries—and the tall, sweet-smelling marram grasses on which Sable's fabled breed of shaggy ponies graze.

The sand is everywhere, beneath the traveller's feet, in his nostrils and hair, and high above him in those strange conical hills—miniature mountains of storm-tossed sand that change their shape continually in the teeth of the wind.

The sand thickens the very waves that crash over those ships unfortunate enough to press too close to the shore. That was the experience of the French corvette *Légère* in June 1746, whose captain believed he was safely past Sable until the sand-choked waves crashed over his bow. He knew at once that the Ile de Sablon was reaching out for him and that there was no escape from its clutches. For the sands of Sable are demonic; they hold their prey in a vicelike grip until it is swallowed by the shoals that lurk a few hundred yards from the beach. The *Légère* went down in September. The remnants of its crew of seventeen castaways were not rescued from Sable until the following June; by that time three had died of scurvy or cold.

The earliest shipwreck of which there is a record was that of the *Delight*, one of Sir Humphrey Gilbert's little fleet brought to the New World in 1583. Trapped in the sand, the vessel began breaking up even before the crew abandoned her. The mountainous waves crashing across her deck washed some men over the side to their deaths, while the currents swirling round the stricken craft created a wall of sand between ship and ocean. In this basin she was able to float for a time until the waters drained away and the clinging sands began to suck the vessel under. Her seams split open; she broke apart and she vanished forever.

Such was the fate of scores of vessels in the days of sail. As one shipwrecked sailor described it three centuries later, "Strong winds and blowing sand exposed

Its back broken, the big four-master Crofton Hall, *cast ashore on Sable Island in April 1898, is imprisoned by the island's clinging sands.*

forty wrecks in a row and when the sand was blown back it uncovered forty more." Bruce Armstrong, in his history of Sable, has described how "wrecks, their bowed ribs like the skeletons of huge prehistoric mammals, support and hold the very sand that destroyed them." The number of ships lost at Sable has been estimated at five thousand. Various maps of the island showing locations of the losses since 1800 depict an astonishing hedgerow of wrecks—four-masters, barques and barquentines, brigs and brigantines, schooners and steamers—encircling the island.

There was a time when the island was part of a great shoal or "bank" that lay between the Grand Banks of Newfoundland and the continent. Exposed during the Ice Age as the sea levels dropped, it began to submerge when the ice melted and the ocean rose again. All the mariner sees today is the tip of the shoal, most of which lies beneath the waves ready to clutch at any vessel that ventures too close to the shore. There are no harbours on the island; it must be approached warily in good weather for, in the words of one observer, it "presents a fifty-mile sandtrap for vessels."

Its geographical position means it attracts disaster. It lies just off the main shipping routes at the point where the chill Labrador Current sweeps down from the north to collide with the warmer Gulf Stream coming up from the south. Thus the island is in the centre of a vortex of conflicting currents that could drive a sailing ship directly onto the grasping sands before anyone realized the danger. These currents are such that bodies from vessels wrecked on the south shore have been whirled around the island crescent to turn up on the north side—macabre swimmers in a grisly marathon.

When the French brigantine *A. S. H.* (known only by its initials) went down in 1884, the corpse of one seaman was found seven miles east of the wreck. One day that same year, as Lyall Campbell explains in his fascinating history of Sable's shipwrecks, an extraordinary current fooled the captain of the S.S. *Amsterdam*. The captain was a veteran of four years of Atlantic crossings. On the basis of observations he had taken the previous day, he thought he was thirty-five miles south of the Sable Island lighthouses. But the Gulf Stream was acting up, and many vessels were thrown off course. Without warning the ship struck Sable's dangerous northeast bar, at least thirteen miles from the nearest likely spot for a safe landing. Six lifeboats battled the surf all night to take off more than two hundred passengers—mostly immigrants—and forty-eight crew members. One boat was swamped before it reached shore, drowning three men. The rest finally made it but were stranded on the island's tip without food for two days before supplies could reach them.

There were times, during the age of sail and before modern communications, when the island was crowded with castaways, some of whom spent months in temporary quarters before rescue ships arrived. In 1825, the only inhabited dwelling was that of Edward Hodgson, superintendent of the Humane Establishment, responsible not only for saving lives and salvaging equipment but also for finding shelter and food for those survivors flung half naked onto the sand.

Most were crowded into Hodgson's house with members of his family, although two other buildings—little more than shacks—were temporarily available. Between September 1825 and May of the following year, Hodgson's home was packed. First, the steamer *Adelphi* went aground, dumping fourteen people on the island, followed a week later by the schooner *Union*, leaving Hodgson to look after eight more. These were no sooner dispatched to the mainland when in January the schooner *Brothers* was driven ashore in a gale. Her captain, six of her crew, and a twelve-month-old baby were saved, but three others perished. They were still crammed into Hodgson's house a month later when the timber ship *Elizabeth* ran aground with eighteen more castaways. None got away until the end of April. Less than a fortnight later the immigrant ship *Nassau* foundered on the northwest bar. Thirty-seven reached the beach, seven more perished, and the remainder stayed aboard the stricken ship. Hard on the heels of this tragedy another timber ship, *Agamemnon*, dumped eighteen more refugees onto the island. Happily there were no more deaths, and eventually all the stranded people, many of whom had lost everything they

Sable Island's Humane Establishment at work with one of its lifeboats in the days when shipwrecks claimed many victims.

owned, were taken to Halifax. The cost to the province of succouring these people was so great that Great Britain stepped in at last and offered to match the amount that Nova Scotia was spending to maintain the hard-pressed Humane Establishment.

No one can tell how many corpses and how many wrecked vessels are hidden by the encroaching sands of Sable. Maritime novelist and historian Thomas Raddall, who worked in Sable's wireless station in 1921, once remarked that to walk across Sable's dunes was like "walking over a big tomb." Old bones lie hidden in the sands and are sometimes uncovered by the wind. After one severe storm in 1963, an island resident came upon the exposed skeleton of a young man who had probably starved to death years before. With the body he found some old British coins dated 1760, half a dozen lead musket balls, and an ancient shoe buckle.

Symbols of death and resurrection recur as the skeletons of ships and men rise out of the sand. In April 1947 the fog was so thick, the winds so furious, the sands so clinging that the Greek freighter *Alfios* could not be freed from the drifts that gripped her when she went aground on an offshore bar. Her crew escaped at the last moment, just before she vanished beneath the Atlantic. Eight years later, on the heels of a savage gale, she suddenly rose like a spectre from her watery grave. For six months she could be clearly seen offshore almost clear of sand. Then, one day, she vanished once again beneath the waves.

Later in 1947 another freighter, *Manhasset*, carrying coal from Newport News, Virginia, to St. John's, was stuck fast on one of Sable's shoals. No rescuing vessel could negotiate the labyrinth of sandbars blocking the way to the stranded ship. The *Manhasset* sank deeper and deeper into the engulfing sands until only her mainmast rose above the waters, its crossbar giving it the image of a grave marker.

Melville Bell Grosvenor saw this macabre landmark when he visited the island in the mid-1960s, lured by the tales told him by his famous grandfather, Alexander Graham Bell. "The Graveyard of the Atlantic," the old inventor had called it, "one of the world's most terrible traps for sailors." Bell had walked these sands in 1898 and told the boy stories of wrecks "littering the beaches," of storms "that undermine the bluffs and scoop out holes in the valleys," and of gales so furious they "made the skin bleed from the impact of fine particles of sand."

In the shallows, some distance down the beach from the crucifix of the *Manhasset*'s mainmast, Grosvenor and his party were startled by another apparition: a headless woman seemed to have risen from the sea, hitching up her skirts. This turned out to be the beautifully carved figurehead of some lost ship, uncovered by the restless sands. She is on display today in a Halifax museum.

There is nothing constant about Sable. Just as ancient vessels have a habit of reappearing, so familiar landmarks are erased by the elements. In his novel *The Nymph and the Lamp*, Thomas Raddall described a house vanishing in drifting sands. The fictional house was based on a real one in which Raddall had lived during his time on the island. The station staff had tried to save it from the encroaching dunes, even building a storm fence to protect it, all to no avail; no amount of shovelling could stop the sand. In the end the dunes buried everything but one attic window.

Sitting as it does at the centre of a whirlpool of warm and cold currents and vagrant gales, Sable is often half hidden by thick fogs or spectral mists that can be as deadly as any phantom. In 1896 the *Raffaele D.*, fifty-four days out of Genoa and bound for Bathurst, New Brunswick, struggled in a fog so dense that her captain could not see the sun and for two days was unable to make any observations. By dead reckoning he believed himself to be thirteen miles east of Sable, but the winds played him false. He was about to take soundings when he saw breakers ahead. Before he could take action the barque struck the island's inner bar and hit the beach broadside. The impact threw her on her beam ends; the main and mizzen masts broke off; the captain became entangled in the rigging and was seriously injured. The Humane Establishment's breeches buoy brought the crew ashore safely but almost did the captain in when it overturned twice in the surf, leaving him all but insensible.

More than one skipper fell victim to Sable's raging waters. In 1853 when the schooner *Guide* was wrecked, the Establishment's lifesaving crew brought all the survivors but one through the high surf. The captain, however, refused point-blank to leave his shattered vessel; his misfortunes had turned him into a "raving maniac," in the words of one witness. By great good fortune, help arrived in the formidable presence of Dorothea Lynde Dix, an American philanthropist and humanitarian who was planning to found an institution for the insane in Halifax. Miss Dix, who was on a brief two-day visit to Sable, arrived on horseback and persuaded the lifesaving crew to return to the stricken schooner, bind the resisting captain hand and foot, and bring him back to shore. This done, she loosened his cords, took him by the arm to a boathouse and, as Bruce Armstrong tells us, "by kind words calmed his mind and persuaded him to thank the sailors for saving his life."

Miss Dix's fortuitous arrival saved more lives than the captain's. When she returned to the United States she raised enough money to buy four new metal lifeboats and modern lifesaving equipment for the island.

It is difficult to estimate the extent of change in Sable over the years because this restless strip of sand is forever transforming its shape, its size, and its position

No one can tell how many corpses and how many wrecked vessels are hidden by the encroaching sands of Sable.

in the Atlantic. For the best part of two centuries it has been moving steadily eastward. In 1634, one shipwrecked sailor, John Rose of Boston, described the island as thirty miles long and two miles broad in places (with a ten-mile lagoon at its midriff). That would make it five miles longer and a mile wider than at present. Some have claimed that it was once two hundred miles long, though that is hard to believe. In the late nineteenth century, Dr. S. D. MacDonald, one of the pioneers of Sable's research, calculated that between 1801 and 1889 the island had shrunk by half. That was probably an exaggeration, as faulty as MacDonald's stated belief that the entire island would soon disappear beneath the ocean.

Sable has not wasted away, but it certainly has changed size and shifted its position over the centuries. We know from early maps that between 1766 and 1900, Sable lost about six miles from its western tip and added nearly six miles to its eastern tip. Half a century later an additional three miles had vanished from the western tail, but the long eastern strip had been extended by more than four. The island has been like a slow-moving barge, easing its way farther into the Atlantic. As a result some of the vessels that left their bones in the shoals that skirt the beaches are now hidden, not by the waves, but beneath the newly shaped island itself.

Those who visit Sable find that they are never free from the sound of the pounding surf—surf so merciless that it can reduce a wooden vessel to kindling, like the beached schooner *Marie Anne*, which, in December 1852, was "beaten into staves" by the sea. On one occasion the surf actually tore the stern off a boat that two seamen were using to escape from the wreck of the Norwegian barque *Gerda*. On that foggy Sunday in June 1890, even though each man was wearing a cork lifebelt, both were too exhausted from battling the waves to reach the shore. A rescue team managed to drag them to safety.

The history of Sable is rife with similar tales of miraculous rescues and near tragedies. One of the most intriguing deals with the wreck of the fishing schooner *Arno*. Trapped, and running out of control in a violent gale with her headsails gone, she was certainly doomed. Her captain had only one choice—a perilous one. He put her before the wind and opted to run her directly onto the shore. First, he ordered all but two of his crew below, nailing up the cabin doors. Then he lashed himself to the helm and ordered the two remaining crew members to roll two large casks of blubber and fish oil forward and rope them into position. Each man was equipped with a two-foot ladle, and both were told to lash themselves to the casks. As the schooner sped before the wind towards the beach, the pair dipped their ladles into the oily mixture and flung the contents as high as possible into the air.

The violent winds carried this combination ahead of the schooner, spreading it over the water, smoothing the surface of the waves and leaving a shining path behind. An eyewitness reported that "the sea was raging, pitching and breaking close to her on each side, but not a barrel of water fell on her deck for the whole distance." The *Arno* struck close to shore and went to pieces, but her crew escaped—a classic and dramatic example of the efficacy of pouring oil on troubled waters.

Today Sable Island is empty of humankind. The lighthouses have been automated, and the Humane Establishment is no longer needed. Visitors to Sable must obtain a hard-to-get permit from the Department of Transport, which administers the island and protects the three-hundred-odd horses that roam the wet sands and feed on the marram grasses, free of hindrance or restraint save that of the harsh winds and the ever-present surf.

The Sable Island lifesaving crew in the 1890s. George Bungay (rear left) and Maurice Norman (rear right) were part of the crew that rescued survivors from the Gerda.

THE MARITIME LOOK

These pictures could only have been taken along the Atlantic coast. White wooden churches and two-masted schooners, rugged cliffs alive with sea birds, lobster dinners, a gabled cottage, a remarkable sea-girt trail, a rock pierced by a great hole—we recognize them all, even if we've never actually been there.

These North American Gothic churches in Mahone Bay, Nova Scotia, are distinctly Maritime in character. From left to right: St. John's Lutheran Church, Trinity United Church, and St. James's Anglican Church.

ABOVE: Volleyballers gambol on the beach at New Brunswick's Miscou Island on the southern shore of the Gulf of St. Lawrence, some forty miles south of Percé.

LEFT: Percé Rock, on the rim of Quebec's Gaspé Peninsula, is perhaps the best-known and most photographed natural feature on the Atlantic coast.

At Cavendish, on the north coast of Prince Edward Island, Japanese tourists by the
hundreds visit the green-gabled home of L. M. Montgomery's redheaded heroine.

ABOVE: *At Nain, a native community on Labrador's ravelled east coast, a cluster of aboriginal moppets pose eagerly for André Gallant's camera.*

LEFT: *The Blessing of the Fleet is a high point of the Acadian Festival held every summer at Caraquet, New Brunswick.*

RIGHT: *Every bird watcher is familiar with the serried cliffs of Bonaventure Island off the Gaspé Peninsula. It harbours one of the largest colonies of gannets in the world.*

Lunenburg Harbour, a popular photo opportunity for tourists, with one of its famous two-masted fishing schooners in the foreground.

ABOVE: Lobster dinners are a P.E.I. specialty as every tourist knows. Here, Katherine Hennessey on the Hillsborough River, not far from Charlottetown, welcomes her guests in the traditional manner.

RIGHT: Few visitors to the Atlantic shore can resist a drive on the Cabot Trail, which winds its way around the northern coast of Cape Breton Island.

Design and Art Direction: Andrew Smith
Page Composition: Andrew Smith Graphics Inc.
Research: Barbara Sears
Consultant: Elsa Franklin
A PETER GODDARD BOOK

ARCHIVAL PICTURE CREDITS